Investing in a Vacation Home for Pleasure and Profit

James H. Boykin, Ph.D., MAI

Australia · Canada · Mexico · Singapore · Spain · United Kingdom · United States

Investing in a Vacation Home for Pleasure and Profit
By James H. Boykin

© 2006 by South-Western, an imprint of Thomson Business and Professional Publishing, a part of the Thomson Corporation. Thomson, the Star logo, South-Western and Thomson Business and Professional Publishing are trademarks used herein.

ISBN: 0-324-31411-6

PCN: 2005922128

Printed and bound in the United States by WestGroup.

2 3 4 5 6 7 07 06 05

For more information, contact Thomson, 5191 Natorp Boulevard, Mason, OH 45040. You can also visit our website at http://realestate.swlearning.com.

Composed by LEAP/International Typesetting and Composition (ITC).

This publication is designed to provide accurate and authoritative information in regard to the subject matter covered. It is sold with the understanding that the publisher is not engaged in rendering legal, accounting, or other professional services. If legal advice or other expert assistance is required, the services of a competent professional person should be sought.

The names of all companies or products mentioned herein are used for identification purposes only and may be trademarks or registered trademarks of their respective owners. South-Western disclaims any affiliation, association, connection with, sponsorship, or endorsement by such owners.

Michele Diehl

BRIEF CONTENTS

Contents

FOREWORD

Investing in a Vacation Home for Pleasure and Profit is a splendid guide for prospective vacation home investors as well as those who already own a resort home. The great appeal of this, Dr. Boykin's latest book, is its logical, comprehensive, and well-researched presentation. Drawing on his successful career as one of America's leading real estate educators, researchers, consultants, and owner of vacation properties, he has produced this marvelous investment book. It is packed with timely advice on the profitable purchase, rental, and sale of a vacation home that should enhance your family's vacationing pleasure as well as your investment portfolio.

The book begins with a discussion of the fundamentals of sound real estate investing, including the benefits and risks of real estate ownership. It will help you evaluate the comparative merits of different types of resorts and determine the ability of different resort locations to satisfy your recreational and cultural desires before and after retirement. It suggests strategies for refining your home search. The book advances through the decisions required in finding your type of "dream home," whether it be in the mountains or by the sea. Advice is offered on timing a purchase and how you should own a home.

Other phases of vacation home investing discussed are selecting a real estate agent and negotiating techniques. How to raise capital for the down payment, mortgage choices, and the steps in financing are thoroughly explained. Covered, too, is the topic of how to protect your investment prior to and after its purchase. The author provides market-tested advice on leasing and exchanging your vacation property after you have settled into your vacation home. Ownership of a vacation home has certain Federal income tax implications, which are discussed at length. Eventually, you may decide to sell your vacation home. This book explains how to maximize your profit by properly preparing it for sale, selecting a broker, and avoiding capital gains taxes on the sale.

Danielle Kennedy
Author of the best-selling title: *"How to List and Sell Real Estate"*
http://www.daniellekennedy.com

Dedication
This book is dedicated with love and
admiration to my sons, Mark and Bruce, and
grandsons, Jonathan, Ben, and
Charlie Boykin.

Acknowledgments

The author acknowledges with deep appreciation the valuable suggestions provided by the following persons: Bryan F. Jones, CPA, Morey, Jones & Pfeiffer, P.C., Richmond, VA; Rick D. Richter, MAI of Richter & Stone, Anchorage, Alaska; William E. Brunson, Brunson Advisors, LLC, Richmond, VA; Christian Gramm and Eric Burgund, Slifer Smith & Frampton Real Estate, Vail, CO; Diana Permar, Permar Inc., Charleston, SC; Andrew Darling, Village Realty, Outer Banks, NC; Karen Timson, Data Research Associates, Breckenridge, CO; Robert W. Taylor, MAI, Virginia Commonwealth University, Richmond, VA; Benjamin Hernandez, Mountain Area Realty, Wintergreen, VA; Cynthia Johnson, SRA, Johnson-Perkins & Associates, Inc., Lake Tahoe, NV; and Mary Martinez, Information Central, National Association of REALTORS®, Chicago, IL.

About the Author

James H. Boykin, Ph.D., MAI, established the Real Estate and Land Development Program at Virginia Commonwealth University, now one of America's most comprehensive real estate programs and currently is serving as Real Estate Professor Emeritus. He has been appointed to a number of posts, including Chairman of the Real Estate Center Directors and Chairholders Association, Regional Vice President and member of the Governing Council of the American Institute of Real Estate Appraisers, Board of Governors of the American Institute of Corporate Asset Management. He was a founding member of the Virginia Appraiser Board and Virginia Commonwealth University Real Estate Foundation Board of Directors. Additionally, he was appointed to the RF&P Corporation Board of Directors (whose real estate assets sold during his board membership for $570 million) and the Real Estate Advisory Committee of the Virginia Retirement System. He presently serves on the Board of Directors of the Ledges Condominium Association at Wintergreen Resort.

He has qualified as an expert real estate witness in 14 courts of law, advised clients nationwide, taught real estate valuation seminars and courses in 29 states, and addressed audiences in numerous places, including Puerto Rico and Northern Ireland. Dr. Boykin has written over 80 real estate articles and authored or been editor of 17 books and monographs on real estate topics, including *Land Valuation Adjustment Procedures and Assignments, The Real Estate Handbook, Mortgage Loan Underwriting, Real Estate Analyses, Financing Real Estate,* and *Real Estate Counseling.* His books and articles have received national awards and are popular among real estate professionals, students, and individual property owners. He frequently is quoted in regional and national media.

He has been recognized in such biographical publications as *Who's Who in the United States, Who's Who in Real Estate, Outstanding Educators of America,* and *Who's Who in Finance and Industry.* Dr. Boykin's contributions to real estate education and industry were recognized in 2002 by the Virginia Association of REALTORS®, the Appraisal Institute (Lifetime

Achievement Award), and by a Joint Resolution issued by the Virginia House of Delegates and Senate.

Dr. Boykin has owned lakefront property and presently owns a mountain ski resort condominium, an ocean resort cottage, as well as an interval ownership.

1 FUNDAMENTALS OF SOUND REAL ESTATE INVESTING

TWO FUNDAMENTAL RULES

Two fundamental rules apply to any type of successful real estate investing. The *first* rule is "Don't lose money," and the *second* rule is "Don't forget the first rule." An investor should remember these cardinal rules for several reasons. If you lose money on your first investment, you may not have the appetite for a second venture, you have wasted hard-earned capital, and you have probably ruined your credit standing so that you may not be able to obtain a mortgage from a bank for several years.

This following rule cannot be overemphasized. It is compelling to think of this touchstone as you consider buying a vacation property: "If you buy real estate wrong, you can't sell it right." Any successful sale of a property depends largely on buying it at a good price. This initial step is essential to your realizing a sizeable profit later when you sell the property.

Establish Your Investment Goals

A good place to begin developing your investment goals is to determine how this investment fits in with your existing investments. Exactly what do you expect ownership of this property to accomplish for you financially? Will it complement your other investments? Will it be a sound building block as you increase your real estate holdings? Will its ownership endanger your ability to stay current on paying your primary home mortgage and maintain your other investments, or will it possibly cause you to liquidate part of your existing portfolio or cause a premature sale of this prospective vacation property at an inopportune time when there are fewer buyers than sellers? Should your strategy be to initially buy a modest property, learn more about property investments in that market, and then trade up to a larger property later that more closely meets your goal of owning a "dream house"?

If you are considering buying a vacation property prior to retirement, how will this house fit in with your lifestyle, income, and savings at that time? Plan ahead, deciding whether it is preferable to pay all cash now or buy it with a mortgage and invest more cash to pay off the loan closer to your retirement.

This analysis requires you to determine whether most of your money can be more productive in alternative investments for a while or whether you are better off by paying cash now. You are faced with a fundamental question: Do you expect to earn more from your securities and other real estate or from the appreciation and rentals from this vacation property? A frank answer to this question will determine whether you liquidate some of your other investments and pay a large down payment (or perhaps all cash) or retain them and place a smaller down payment on the cottage or chalet.

Three Principal Benefits of Owning Real Estate

The principal benefits that are possible through real estate ownership are (1) **equity buildup,** (2) **rental income,** and (3) **income tax shelter.** The initial equity in a real estate investment is the down payment. This assumes that the sales price does not exceed the appraised value. For example, if the property is worth $200,000 and you paid $185,000, you automatically have an initial equity of $15,000. The amount of equity changes as the value of the property changes. You want to be assured after studying recent price trends and understanding future influences on value that your investment will increase and not decline. The other influence on the change in equity value is the amount that the mortgage is reduced (amortized) in the future. Figure 1.1 illustrates how equity can increase from these two factors.

Assume that an investor has an initial investment of $75,000, which is a 25 percent down payment on a $300,000 home. The loan is a 6 percent, monthly installment, 25-year term mortgage. The property is expected to increase in value by 5 percent annually. Thus, after 25 years when the $225,000 loan has been repaid, the equity rises to $1.016 million. Stated

Figure 1.1
Equity buildup from property appreciation and loan amortization.

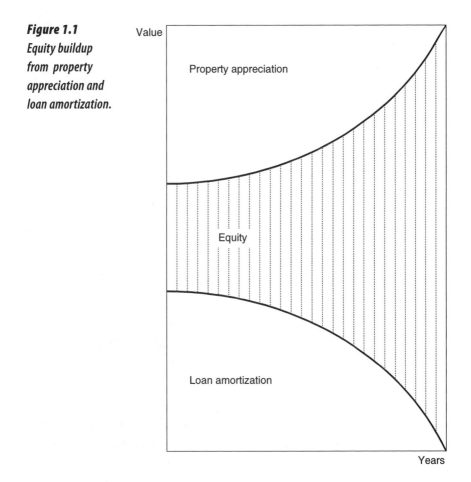

Value

Property appreciation

Equity

Loan amortization

Years

differently, the original down payment has increased at an annual rate of nearly 11 percent. Of course, if the property appreciates at a faster rate, then the investor's equity grows at an even more rapid rate.

Rental income usually is a major benefit of owning **improved real estate,** which is a site with a building on it in contrast to a vacant site. Rental income from vacation property falls somewhere between incomes from an improved investment property with year-around rentals, such as an apartment building, and vacant land, which usually produces no rentals. This is because some owners don't want to rent their property and others who chose to do so find that their lake or beach house rentals have a very busy peak season of three plus months, an off season, and modest rental activity during the shoulder seasons. Thus, the rental income benefit is not as significant as for commercial, apartment, and retail properties. It is important to make a realistic projection of how much rental income is likely, especially if you need it to offset some or all of the mortgage payments, real estate taxes, utilities, condominium association fees, furnishings, decorating, and **repairs.**

Real estate investments with a high ratio of depreciable asset value to total property value can provide significant tax shelter for income from other sources. This is where the building(s) value is relatively high. For example, a property is acquired for $500,000, and the building (which can be depreciated for income tax purposes) is worth $400,000. This benefit may not be as important for vacation property as will be explained in Chapter 15.

IDENTIFY OWNERSHIP RISKS

Some of the risks inherent in owning real estate are as follows:

❖ *Renovation and refurbishing expenditures.* It is generally more difficult to accurately estimate renovation costs than it is to gauge new construction costs. This is especially true for termite and other wood-boring insect damage, electrical improvements, and upgrades to plumbing within the interior walls. Of course, you will want to include a provision for termite inspection if termite activity is prevalent in your area, as well as inspections of electrical and plumbing systems, **HVAC,** roofing, asbestos, and for determining the dwelling's structural soundness. At the same time, you should obtain cost estimates from qualified contractors to make the necessary repairs and upgrades.

✤ *Market timing.* Unquestionably, real estate markets are cyclical. However, these cycles tend to be long term, so you could easily await for a downturn so that you can buy a vacation property for your family at a lower price only to find that by the time it occurs, your children have left home. It is also possible, even with a downturn, that the prices will be above the present level. Many people have delayed the purchase of a **vacation home** either to wait for a downturn or until they have saved enough money to buy a cottage. When they later return to their favorite resort, they are shocked at how high the prices have soared. For example, in 2003, a 1,200-square-foot cabin on Lake Tahoe, Nevada, may have cost over $3 million. The message is: "Waiting won't make a property cheaper." In fact, property prices may rise faster than your savings.

✤ *Rent risk.* This risk is of greatest concern for buyers who already have sizeable mortgage payments on their primary home and other consumer bills. They may have purchased the vacation home anticipating rental income sufficient to offset much of their mortgage payments, insurance, real estate taxes, repairs, and replacements. This can be a risky situation and is best overcome by using the existing rental list to contact past renters, using the same rental company if its fees and performance are acceptable, and setting aside enough money to cover at least six months of operating expenses. By then, the property should produce substantial offsetting income.

✤ *Overpaying for the property.* This particular risk can be managed. As you begin your property search, go to an Internet search engine. Enter a query such as "Naples Florida real estate companies." This should display several real estate brokerage firms, some of which also manage rental properties. Next, set the parameters of your property search. For example, you may give the price range from $300,000 to $500,000; minimum number of bedrooms at 3; and minimum number of baths at 3. Next, identify communities of interest or perhaps waterfront or other choices. This search will help acquaint you with properties in your price range and begin to familiarize you with asking prices of similar homes. Your **real estate agent** can assist in this manner also, plus provide the comparable sales that he used in establishing the listing price on a property. Once you find a property that you like, make a reasonable offer under the asking price. Finally, make the purchase contingent on the loan appraisal being at least as high as the contract price.

✤ *Property use risk.* You want to be absolutely certain that you can use the property fully once you have purchased it. Check to determine if you can use it without any zoning restrictions. I recall once looking at a mountain property on which an addition had been made to the house. This addition encroached about three feet into the side yard setback requirement. For other reasons, I decided not to buy the property, but this zoning violation would needed to have been resolved by the seller as a condition to my buying the property. Similarly, there may be building height violations, e.g., blocking a scenic view from other nearby properties. Another potential violation is when electrical or plumbing work has been done without the required municipal permits and inspections. If such a problem is discovered, place the burden on the seller to rectify it before closing on the purchase. In low-lying areas without public sewer systems, septic drain field failure during rainy seasons can be a major problem. Have the local health department check out the system and well water quality for compliance. Find out if there are any environmental issues affecting the property. These could come from hazardous waste migrating from another property via an underground stream onto your prospective vacation property. Finally, check to determine whether you can obtain **flood insurance** at an affordable rate and legally enlarge the house.

OBJECTIVELY EVALUATE YOUR PRESENT FINANCIAL CONDITION

The starting point in evaluating your net worth[1] is to review your personal financial statements from the past five years. From this analysis, you can trace overall trends, as well as these individual components:

✤ How much has your net worth grown annually and overall over the past five years?

✤ How are your assets distributed between liquid and fixed assets?

✤ Is your investment portfolio designed to achieve your financial goals, or is it just a random and illogical collection of assets?

✤ Are your assets structured to achieve financial security?

---

[1] **Net worth** is the amount that assets exceed **liabilities**. Assets may be free and clear or encumbered by debt. The cash value of insurance policies, not the much larger face value, would be included as an asset. **Liquid assets** can readily be converted into cash and include bank accounts, stocks, bonds, and the cash value of insurance policies. Nonliquid assets cannot easily be converted into cash for the down payment. These include other real estate, automobiles, and possibly retirement accounts. Included under liabilities are unpaid debts.

- ✤ Do you have ample liquid assets to cover diminished rentals in the off-season and property upgrades on the prospective vacation property?

- ✤ How will you make the real estate taxes, insurance, and mortgage payments?

- ✤ How large and what is the nature of your liabilities?

- ✤ What is the dollar amount of your cash assets? Are they sufficient for the property's down payment? If not, which of the remaining assets can readily be converted to cash, and is the penalty or early withdrawal fee acceptable?

- ✤ Do you anticipate that your salary income and income from investments will be adequate to stay current on your other expenditures plus the new vacation property—even in retirement?

Set Clear and Achievable Investment Goals

As you consider the various options for owning a vacation property, ask yourself whether owning this home will contribute to your overall investment goals. You need to set down on paper your overall investment goals and then create a time line toward achieving these goals. Note where you stand along this continuum now, where you expect to be next year, in five years, etc. As part of this planning process, determine how and if owning a vacation property will positively impact your goals.

Simply stating a goal does not begin to make it happen. Ask yourself several questions: Is this an achievable goal? Can we reasonably achieve the desired outcome? Are we willing to take on the accompanying risk and personal sacrifices necessary for its financial success? Moreover, will we enjoy ourselves during the building, remodeling, leasing, and management stages?

An essential component to achieving your vacation property investment goals is to state them in a clear, straightforward manner. Two things should occur as you refine the investment goals for your prospective property. First, the goals will become clearer and better defined. If you cannot clearly and succinctly express your goals, you certainly won't understand them, and as a result, will never achieve them. Second, by refining your goals, you will realize that your first several attempts probably were crude and not achievable. Additionally, any of these earlier half-baked plans could have produced dire financial results.

Never allow your ego to outweigh an objective analysis of the facts concerning a potential real estate investment. Although you may "fall in love" with a particular vacation property, the purchase must be sensible or, all too quickly, you will regret your new acquisition. Rely on others who are experts in their respective fields to temper your first impression. Once they have been contacted, ask for and check on references from their prior clients. Some people will request references but fail to follow up with telephone inquiries of these clients.

There is a natural tendency to be overly optimistic in estimating rent and occupancy levels and to underestimate expenditures. Remember, "paper" profits cannot be deposited at your bank. This is what I call "wishing your way to success," and it doesn't work. Moreover, this illusion of success likely will lead to disappointment later. If you err in your forecasts, it is far better to be conservative in order to allow sufficient time for repairs and leasing, downturns in local real estate sales and rental activity, periods of overbuilding, and weakness in the economy. Similarly, by being conservative rather than overly optimistic in setting your goals, you will more likely set aside sufficient reserves to bring the property along to achieve your pleasure and profit goals.

Realistically Judge Your Capabilities

Never overestimate your capability to comprehend renter preferences; structural soundness of the building and its HVAC, electrical, and plumbing systems; legal nuances in a purchase contract or lease; limitations imposed by the zoning code or environmental controls; physical features of the site; or neighborhood resistance to change (**NIMBY**, that is, "not in my backyard"). Research the market and property thoroughly prior to making an offer to purchase it. Locate the appropriate tradesmen and real estate professionals to assist with your **due diligence**. They can be of immense help in not only pointing out flaws in the property but also in showing you how apparently serious problems may have a fairly simple and inexpensive solution. They may be able to do some of the repair and renovation work later. Even though you have become familiar with these tradesmen, nevertheless obtain several proposals for any project on the house.

To obtain municipal approval for repair work, generally you will need licensed workers. Without using licensed workers, you may not be able to get approvals from the town. It is especially crucial to hire licensed electricians to avoid electrical system failures, which may cause house fires. If the work was performed by an unlicensed electrician, the insurance company may refuse to pay your claim. There are times when you cannot afford cheap labor and materials.

To illustrate the problem of overestimating your capability to perform repair and renovation work, a homeowner called a plumber to finish a job that he had started and was unable to complete. The plumber at first said that it would cost $300 to install the plumbing. Attempting to reduce the price the homeowner said that he had already started the job. On hearing this, the plumber said, "Oh, in that case it will cost you $500."

USING LEVERAGE

Leverage is the result of borrowing capital for an investment. The key thing for you to remember is that *leverage multiplies financial results*. It may be either positive or negative. For a strictly income-producing investment, there is positive leverage when the cash flow is positive. That is, there is positive income after all the property operating expenses and the mortgage payments have been paid. However, a rental vacation property generally will not produce positive cash flow. Hence, it generally is wise to use less leverage (debt) than would be typical for a commercial or retail investment property.

Never overestimate your financial capacity to carry a real estate investment during (1) the initial period needed to build up a stable rent roll, (2) slack rental seasons, (3) overly competitive future markets, or (4) a downturn in the leasing market or general economy.

At least initially, it would be prudent to obtain a conservative mortgage loan on a vacation property. By investing more equity in the form of a larger down payment, your mortgage payments will be less and protect your investment if rental income declines, the economy sours, weather conditions deter tourism and in turn reduce rental activity, or if operating expenses and repairs rise unexpectantly. Another reason to avoid thin equity (via low down payment) is that in addition to increasing your monthly mortgage payments, you may have sharply rising expenses unrelated to the vacation property, which could affect your ability to retain the property. You certainly don't want to lose this property because of your inability to stay current on the mortgage payments, insurance, real estate taxes, and repairs.

2 IMPACT OF BOOMERS AND ECONOMY ON VACATION HOMES

DEMOGRAPHIC TRENDS

The affluent **Baby Boomers** are just entering the peak age for purchasing resort and second homes.[2] They are both the largest and wealthiest single population group in history. These are Americans who were born between 1946 and 1964. In 2005, their ages ranged from 41 to 59. They are slated to inherit more than $12 trillion over the next 16 years. "By the time Americans have reached pre-retirement age of 55 to 64 years, they are 65 percent more likely than all other adults to own a **second home**."[3] The demand generated by this group will not falter until 2015 when the oldest reach 70 years. As this generation begins to pass wealth to their children, estimated to be a multi-trillion-dollar intergenerational

---

[2] The term "second home" includes both vacation and investment homes rather than a person's primary residence.

[3] Dean Schwanke, et al., Urban Land Institute *Resort Development Handbook*, (Washington, DC: ULI-the Urban Land Institute, 1997) p. 380.

transfer of capital assets, another round of demand for second homes should occur.

The Baby Boomer market is some 76 million strong and represents about 30 percent of the U.S. population. According to Urban Land Institute's "Market Views," "By 2005, 40 percent of this group will have an individual net worth exceeding $500,000 and an annual income of more than $100,000."[4] The prior generation, known as the Silent Generation (born between 1925 and 1945), still plays a role in the vacation market. As of 2005, the younger one-half of that group ranged from 60 to 70 years and typically had recently retired or was approaching retirement. Of course, many of these people will be selling or giving their second homes to Boomers.

Dave Morrison, a Caldwell Banker **REALTOR**® in Miami, Florida, found that Baby Boomers had a major influence on the vacation property market because: "(1) they have the economic clout and more disposable income than any other age segment, (2) as Baby Boomers mature, the children are graduating from college and the financial burden of tuition is lifted, (3) . . . they are willing to pay top dollar if they are getting value for their money, (4) Boomers view buying properties in resort communities as an investment opportunity, and (5) many Boomers are looking toward vacation home buying to fulfill both the short- and long-term goals of vacationing and retirement living."[5]

According to demographer Peter Francese, founder of *American Demographics*, Americans are expected to buy 3.6 million second homes over the next decade or about 1,000 a day. This will bring the total number of individuals owning these properties to over 10 million. He goes on to note, "During this decade, the fastest rising age group will be the 55- to 64-year-olds, the age cohort with the highest propensity to own a second home—nearly 1 in 10 of these households own one. As Baby Boomers take over that age group, the projected increase of 7 million households in the 55 to 64 age category—combined with just 1 percent increase in their propensity to own two places—would mean an additional 1 million homes."[6]

---

[4] ULI-the Urban Land Institute *Urban Land*, "Market Views" (August 2002), p. 50.
[5] Lee Stephens, "Vacation Home Buying Season Is Fueled by Baby Boomer Demand," an Internet article quoting Dave Morrison.
[6] Peter Francese, "The Coming Boom in Second-Homeownership," *American Demographics* (October 2001), p. 27.

"Independent and often wireless workers are also expected to fuel this anticipated rise in second-homeownership. . . . If going to the office becomes less important, more of these workers may spend additional days working from their vacation retreats. . . . Locations that are equipped with superior phone service and that offer high-speed Internet services may find demand for second homes exceeding that for year-round use."

Since the horridly savage terrorist attacks in New York on September 11, 2001, many urban dwellers have sought to "escape" to quiet, scenic, and serene places not too distant from their primary residences. One resort agent stated that immediately after 9/11 his telephone "rang off the hook." In a number of resorts, inventory of vacation properties fell to low levels with prices rising sharply. This trend was already underway as the Baby Boomers were beginning to reach their prime second home buying ages.

WHO BUYS VACATION HOMES?

About half of the nearly 6 million existing second homes are used for seasonal recreation use, and the other half are held for rental investment property. Second home buyers tend to be married and older than other home buyers. The U.S. Bureau of the Census reports that seasonal homeownership continues to rise—from 1.7 million in 1980 to 3.6 million in the third quarter of 2002.

If there is a typical second home buyer, it is a married, middle-class Baby Boomer. The 2003 *National Association of REALTORS® Profile of Home Buyers and Sellers* survey indicated that at 47 years, the median age of these buyers was seven years older than the typical home buyer. They also earned a higher median income in 2002: $85,900 versus $66,300. Second home owning households were more likely to be married couple families than other home buying households and less likely to have children at home. It should be noted from this survey that only about 10 percent of the recently purchased second homes were in a resort or recreation area.

The latest NAR survey found that 51 percent of second home buyers plan to keep their property as a vacation retreat, 18 percent purchased for retirement, 16 percent bought to diversify their investments, and 15 percent sought rental income from their second home. Forty percent of second home buyers live in the suburbs, while 22 percent come from small towns, followed by 18 percent from urban areas.

It was found that most vacation homes are located within a median distance of 185 miles from their owner's principal home. One-third were situated more that 500 miles from the owner's primary residence, and another one-third were less than 100 miles from the owner's main home. The comparative value of these vacation homes is just $50,000 less than the value of their $200,000 primary homes.

Robert Freedman, writing in a March 2000 *REALTOR® Magazine Online* article "Grabbing a Ray of Sunshine," asserts that most second home buyers come from cities and buy vacation homes in rural areas. He quotes an American Housing Survey that found that "Half of all second homes are located in rural areas, compared to 14 percent of primary residences. About 44 percent of all vacation homes are in Texas and Florida. California is popular as well as New York's Catskill Mountains and Michigan."

Vacation home buyers are very deliberate. Typically, they buy after their third visit to an area. According to Gee Dunston of Ocean City, Maryland, it takes them 28 months to make a purchase versus 90 days for primary home purchasers.[7]

How Strong Is the Vacation Home Market?

The latest U.S. Census estimates that there are about 8 million second homes, including condominiums and time-shares. Of these, about 3.5 million are recreational properties according to the National Association of REALTORS® (Figure 2.1 depicts an upscale ski resort home). The large number of people in their 40s and 50s entering the vacation home market could very well fuel an additional 100,000 to 150,000 housing starts every year through 2010. This age group represents people entering both their peak earning and vacation home purchasing years. Those in the 55- to 64-year age bracket are the second largest second home buyers group.

It is expected that there will be a strong upsurge in demand for second homes in the 2000–2010 period. Fueling this demand up tick is the convergence of a demographic age bubble of maturing adults who are affluent. Working professionals, after suffering through three years of stock market losses, still have considerable personal wealth and more to come through inheritance. Also, they have sizeable equity in their primary

---

[7] "Home Sweet Home," *Real Estate Business* (May/June 2001), p. 26.

Figure 2.1
Ski Resort home in Bachelor Gulch, Colorado.

Courtesy of Mike Bradbury at Slifer Smith & Frampton Real Estate, Vail, Colorado.

residence, which can be accessed via sale, refinancing, or deferred tax exchanges. They have the ability and desire to work away from the traditional office setting at least several days a week. The idea of working in a relaxed, scenic, resort-type environment has become increasingly appealing. It has encouraged many pre-retirees to acquire vacation/retirement homes before retiring. A "work" day may be divided between typical office work (in shorts and sport shirt versus suit and tie) and leisure activities such as reading, hiking, golfing, swimming, sunning on the beach, or visiting nearby wineries and quaint shops.

STOCKS, BONDS, PRINCIPAL RESIDENCES, AND SECOND HOME VALUES

The punishing losses of the U.S. stock markets between March 24, 2000, and July 18, 2002 (falling nearly 42 percent), have left some investors fearful of investing aggressively in securities any time soon. Some of these investors have kept their greatly diminished holdings in securities but are placing new investments in fixed tangible assets such as real estate, especially vacation homes. During the first seven months of 2004, the stock market was erratic with investors jittery about record-high oil prices and ongoing threats from terrorists. The Dow Jones Index was off by 25 percent and the Nasdaq down by 65 percent over the past three years, while vacation property values were up 15 percent annually or more in some prime resort markets.

Home prices are up sharply in some markets such as Cape Cod, Massachusetts (+64%); Cape May, New Jersey (+56%); Lake Tahoe, California (+52%); Sarasota County, Florida (+37%); and Jupiter Island, Florida (+37%). According to David Stiff with Fiserv CSW, Census Bureau statistics showed that in these and other counties with a high proportion of vacation homes, home values increased overall by 37 percent between the second quarters of 2000 and 2003. Similarly, the Orinda, CA-based *EscapeHomes.com*'s Price Index for Second Homes surveyed select vacation home markets and found that single family detached home prices in these markets rose by 22 percent between the second quarters of 2003 and 2004.[8] This appreciation was more than double the 9 percent rates reported by the National Association of REALTORS® and the National Association of Home Builders. Similar results can be seen over a longer term in the table on page 16 where all three classes of recreation property surpass the gains of stocks with the DJIA up 56 percent since 1996, long-term Treasury bonds rose 63 percent, and primary homes were up 48 percent during this period.[9] Not surprisingly, some investment portfolios have been adjusted to include resort properties that families see increasing in value and that can be used for their personal pleasure. Vacation home price trends can vary significantly among resorts. For example, on the Outer Banks of North Carolina, prices more than tripled between 1999 and mid-2004—partly because larger, more expensive homes were built. Rising costs of land, materials, and labor, plus strong demand, have forced prices up in many areas. However, sometimes overall prices may decline when a higher proportion of lower-priced condominiums are built and sold.

The following is an overview of price trends in selected U.S. resorts. In Summit County, Colorado, home of Breckenridge ski resort, average prices climbed 252 percent from 1988 to mid-2004 and rose 67 percent since

[8] Broderick Perkins, "Values in Select Second Home Markets Up 22 Percent," *Realty Times* (August 16, 2004). The markets surveyed by EscapeHomes.com were Bend, OR; Holden Beach, NC; Incline Village, NV; Myrtle Beach, NC; Naples, FL; Park City, UT; Santa Barbara, CA; Sarasota, FL; St. Helena, CA; and Truckee, CA.

[9] Brunson Advisors, LLC, Professional Asset Management for Investors (Richmond, VA) and "Median Sales Price of Existing Single-Family Homes," National Association of REALTORS® (Washington, DC).

1996. Similarly, resort home prices in Vail Valley, Colorado, rose 268 percent since 1988 and were up 99 percent since 1996.[10] In Virginia's Wintergreen all-season mountain resort, after prices were flat for several years, they rose 79 percent between 1998 and mid-year 2004.[11] Rosemary Beach (in Florida's Panhandle) resale homes rose from $437,000 to $871,000 between 1997 and mid-2004, or 99 percent.[12]

Some interesting comparisons can be seen between the comparative price trends of resales of detached homes, villas (multi-family structures), and lots between 1996 and mid-2004:

Resort	Type of Real Estate		
	Detached Homes	Villas (multi-family)	Lots
Kiawah Island, SC	+207%	+109%	+229%
Palmetto Dunes, SC	+99%	+148%	+278%
Seabrook Island, SC	+150%	+152%	+402%
Wild Dunes, SC	+167%	+162%	+182%

Source: Diana Permar, Permar Inc. (Charleston, SC).

The above illustrative sample of resorts suggests that (1) detached home prices perform slightly better than condominiums and (2) lot price appreciation generally out-performs improved property gains by a substantial margin. Remember, however, that lots generate no income and only limited income tax benefits compared to vacation homes.

A significant stimulus for vacation home demand was passage of the 1997 tax law change which allowed couples to exclude up to $500,000 in capital gains from the sale of their primary residence. (This topic is developed fully in Chapter 15.) Some of these sellers used part of the sale proceeds to buy a vacation home, and some even did so with the intention of acquiring a vacation home prior to moving in it after they retire. An NAR study indicated that about 30 percent of all buyers expect to convert their second homes to their primary homes sometime in the future.

---

[10] Karen Sue Davis, Data Research Associates (Breckenridge, CO).
[11] Benjamin W. Hernandez, Mountain Area Realty (Wintergreen, VA).
[12] Diana Permar, Permar Inc. (Charleston, SC).

INFLUENCES ON RESORT PROPERTY DEMAND

Well-located and attractive land will continue to be constrained by such factors as rising development costs and environmental restrictions. Increasingly, prime resort development land is being reserved for conservation purposes. As this trend coincides with rising demand for resort property by Baby Boomers and Echo Baby Boomers (**Generation X**—those born between 1965 and 1978), the value of such properties will continue to rise.

Many people across all income and age groups now look to their resort homes, especially those homes in rural areas, as safe havens for themselves, their family, and friends to relax. Since the 9/11 terrorist attack on the World Trade Center, mid-market buyers have placed even more emphasis on owning vacation property within a convenient three- to four-hour driving distance from their principal residence. In fact, the National Association of REALTORS® has found that most vacation properties already are within a half-day's drive of their primary residence, half are located in rural areas, and just 10 percent are in central cities. These convenient locales will be more popular among those who want to avoid the extra expense, trouble, and delays of commercial airline travel.

The lack of state personal income taxes can increase the appeal of one state over another state. For example, California has a personal income tax, while the adjoining state, Nevada, has no state income tax. Moreover, it has no inheritance tax and comparatively low real estate taxes. The result is strong demand for both retirement and vacation homes in Nevada. The absence of state income taxes can boost demand and real estate prices in such low-tax areas as around Lake Tahoe, which is partially in each state.

Increasingly, resort property purchasers are expecting more than a home in a golfing community. In fact, the golf population seems to be in a flat growth pattern. If golf is desired, it must be a quality experience, but it is just one piece of the overall recreation experience that also embraces desired soft amenities such as education, cultural, and other indoor and outdoor experiences. In effect, buyers are expecting a "full package" of year-round amenities. These may include fishing, hiking, biking, downhill and cross-country skiing, water skiing, kayaking, swimming, tennis, and nature centers and trails (Figure 2.2 shows a couple enjoying bicycling in the mountains).

Courtesy of Wintergreen Resort, Wintergreen, Virginia.

Figure 2.2
Bicyclists enjoying view of Blue Ridge Mountains.

Increasing numbers of vacationers seek authentic natural environments where they can learn about and appreciate the natural environment. Developments that have maintained a community's natural beauty are appealing to the ecotourist. They seek out resorts where the tranquility of natural settings has been disturbed only minimally. Mountains and rivers are preserved, and beaches are not overwhelmed by high-rise towers.

3 WHAT YOU WANT IN A VACATION HOME

Take inventory of what you enjoy most on your vacations. Are there some outdoor activities that you want to cultivate? Have your cultural and recreational interests changed in recent years? What would you enjoy most in your vacation home and resort in future years? Does the prospective community possess the assets you desire, and will you be comfortable with the people who will be your neighbors? What is its policy toward protection of the environment? How do you plan to use the home, and will this change before and after you retire? By answering these questions, you will begin to create a framework from which you can visualize where you want to buy a vacation home and what features you want in a neighborhood and home.

You should determine whether the municipality has a lax development policy. That is, does it welcome unfettered residential development that may compete against the property that you plan to purchase and later rent and resell? If there is little available developable land or a stringent municipal development policy, the tight housing supply should boost the rental demand and value of your property.

The majority of vacation homeowners want to be close to an ocean, river, or lake (76 percent), followed by those who want to be close to their favorite vacation area (37 percent), and 38 percent who want to be close to mountains or other natural attractions.[13] This desire to be near the water explains the strong price appreciation of water-oriented vacation properties.

Increasingly, ski resorts are developing and marketing year-around activities for property owners and guests. Some observers note that, "They come for the winter and stay for the summer." Many favor the off-peak season with its smaller crowds and pleasant relief from the hot weather at lower elevations back home.

Mountain biking has become a popular summer activity in mountain ski resorts. Chair lifts are refitted to carry bikes and riders up the mountain so they can descend on bike paths as well as provide sightseeing rides. Hikers may also use the chair lifts to reach summits and then hike down the mountain. Many mountain resorts now aggressively promote summer conferences and concert series.

LOCATION, DEMAND, AND VALUE

Access to desired leisure activities probably is the strongest influence for buying recreation property. While vacation homes are found in all of the states, the majority are located in Florida, California, Texas, and Michigan, followed by Maine, Vermont, New Hampshire, Alaska, Delaware, Florida, Arizona, Wisconsin, Montana, and Hawaii. Initially, you should determine where you want to be and then refine your choice to provide the desired amenities and type and price of property that fit your needs and budget.

A river or creek frontage lot's value can be significantly impaired by three accessibility factors: channel location, silting, and low bridges. A narrow, twisting channel can present navigation problems for a person attempting to reach a property. Moreover, if the channel is on the opposite side of the body of water, there may be mud flats between it and your lot, which can limit your boating and swimming. Channels often will silt in, greatly restricting the size of boat that can reach a lot. A prospective lot or home buyer must always know what barriers exist downstream from a particular property. The presence of a low bridge, overhead power line, or a boat

---

[13] *The 2002 National Association of REALTORS® Profile of Second-Homeowners* (Chicago: National Association of REALTORS®, 2003). Used with permission.

tunnel under a road can severely restrict the size of boat that otherwise could access an upstream lot, greatly reducing its appeal and value.

River, Bay, Ocean, Lake, Mountains, or Golfing Community

This book focuses on resort property because it is easier and generally more profitable to rent homes in these locations to renters than in remote areas. Professional rental and property management firms are readily available to assist you. Prospective renters and eventually buyers are more aware of and seek homes in established resorts rather than in isolated places lacking support services and transportation. Further, you are able to achieve higher rankings for property exchanges.

Mountain Ski Resort

Urban Land Institute notes that, "Technology has made it possible to build facilities in locations where, without snow making, the ski season would last less than a week. In most regions, though, a ski area needs a combination of natural and artificial snow that permits about 80 to 100 days of skiing."[14] There are four types of ski resorts:

- *Type I resorts*—These international destinations feature excellent mountains and a wide variety of lodging and real estate.

- *Type II resorts*—These resorts are not as well known in the marketplace as Type I resorts; they offer fewer activities and appeal to a more limited market, such as ski clubs and groups.

- *Type III resorts*—These resorts offer high-quality skiing but little real estate development. Many operate only on weekends.

- *Small, often marginal developments*—These resorts operate only on weekends. For example, the typical club hill in Ontario has no snow making, less than a 300-foot drop, and a T-bar lift and a chalet without a liquor license.[15]

---

[14] Dean Schwanke, et al., *Resort Development Handbook* (Washington, DC: ULI-the Urban Land Institute, 1997), p. 150.

[15] Robert Christie Mill, *Resorts—Management and Operation* (New York: John Wiley & Sons, Inc., 2001), p. 120.

Not everyone visits ski resorts to ski. For example, "Thirty percent of winter visitors at Vail, Colorado, do not ski. At Tremblant, Quebec and Whistler, British Columbia, non-ski activities have become so popular that skiers may find it difficult to find hotel rooms in the middle of winter."[16] Nonskiers enjoy the winter scenery as well as the spa. In fact, health conscious travelers are attracted to well-appointed spas throughout the year. In virtually every ski resort, homeowners are buying a lifestyle, not just housing. A five-year hold for a residence is typical.

Aspen was an old mining town and began as a ski resort in 1948. It has relatively little ski-in/ski-out (SI/SO) opportunities. A property offering this feature might command a 10 to 20 percent premium. Nearby snowmass has more SI/SO and is more family oriented—maybe a 3 to 10 percent premium would be expected for the SI/SO feature.

The strongest part of the market in Aspen is the $1–2 million home, so a person looking for a $300,000–$400,000 home likely would need to look elsewhere. Snowmass is less expensive, family oriented, and offers more beginner and intermediate slopes. The high-end part of the market is not as subject to changing economic conditions as the lower end of the market. High-end buyers often aren't interested in renting their homes even though four- to five-bedroom homes usually are popular rentals. Buyers are most interested in dwelling size and access to the slopes.

Buyer Priorities

1. Popular locations are within comfortable walking distance (with skis) to lifts near the village. Slope settings are viewed as 100 percent locations. Prices may decline as much as 50 percent if the walk to the slopes is over five minutes. Unique locations, such as **ski-in/ski-out sites**, command premium prices. Ski-in/ski-out sites generally are defined as those within 50–100 yards of a slope or gondola.

2. Three- and four-bedroom units are popular, with one and two bedrooms having less appeal. Larger homes are important for buyers who enjoy periodically gathering with their families at a resort. The size of the unit is important, as well as availability of ski storage. You shouldn't expect many single-family detached dwellings to have the ski-in/ski-out convenience.

---

[16] Gregory Ochis, et al., "Destination East," *Urban Land* (August 1999), p. 31.

3. The most popular home sites in Vail are on the ski slopes with exciting unobstructed "hard rock" views; the Gore range vista is quite popular.

4. Penthouses with vaulted ceilings are prime properties.

5. Assigned parking for townhouses/condos is an asset in congested areas. Covered parking is especially appealing for mountain resort property.

A south-facing condominium with ski slope views may bring $800 a square foot, while a north-facing unit in the same building without the view may command only $400 a square foot (in 2002). Buyers will pay a lot for the best in a world-class resort but not much for an inferior product.

Caveats to Buyers

1. Determine the most popular building orientation, such as southerly (south facing) in the Rocky Mountains, to gain more sun exposure and warmth in the winter.

2. Select a unique location, such as ski-in/ski-out. There won't be many new ski resorts developed in the future due to constraining environmental regulations and high capital requirements. Therefore, values of these prime locations will rise handsomely in the future.

3. Condominiums vary in price by elevation in a building and by view. For example, in Antlers at Vail, similar two-bedroom units vary from the base price as follows: third floor, 100 percent; fourth floor, 102 percent; fifth floor, 104 percent.

4. A strong, well-capitalized owner-developer is important to sustain high-quality services.

5. Look for a resort that has reliable skiing conditions.

6. Properties in popular resorts can expect rising prices. Buy in a resort where people will want to visit. Vail has seen more price run-up in the past decade than in any previous decade since opening in 1962. Other popular ski resorts include Whistler, Aspen, Vail, Killington, Mount Snow, Jackson Hole, Cataloochee, Winter Park, and Squaw Valley.

7. Weigh condo dues against the amenities provided.

8. Determine the level of past assessments and whether future assessments are expected to rise sharply.

9. Avoid vehicular traffic noise and insufficient parking. Check for sound insulation between living units.

10. Locate close to a shuttle bus line.

11. Ski-in/ski-out sites are superior to a village location.

12. Consider the property's maintenance cost, including siding replacement.

Demand may be equal for units on beginners versus intermediate slopes. However, the first preference is a ski-in/ski-out dwelling, which is within 50–60 yards of a slope or lift. Some owners and renters don't mind being off the slopes since prices and rents are lower, especially if there is reliable, frequent shuttle service to the slopes. Hot tubs are preferred and frequently requested.

Whistler, British Columbia, began developing back in the early '60s when the closest village was Alta Lake, a tiny fishing resort. Today, it frequently is ranked as the number one ski resort in North America and even worldwide. Whistler, or Whistler/Blackcomb in recognition of the adjoining mountains, is two hours from Vancouver. It is the largest resort in North America, with over 7,000 acres of skiable terrain, more than 200 trails, 12 bowls, 3 glaciers, and 33 lifts. Blackcomb's vertical rise is one mile, and Whistler's is just slightly less. Its ski season sometimes stretches out to the end of May.

As you screen each different resort as a place to visit and maybe even retire to, keep in mind its popularity. Generally, as a resort's fame increases so do the property values within it. For example, Whistler has about 16,000 daily visitors in the winter and 13,000 in the summer. Whistler is big, with more than 200 shops and over 90 restaurants; it offers a variety of entertainment after sundown. The average price of home sales rose from $274,943 (Canadian) in 1990 to $553,942 in 2000. RE/MAX of Whistler reported that in 2002 prices of homes were up 34 percent and condo prices rose by 18 percent. Over the past 13 years, according to Barb Cofield of RE/MAX Whistler, overall property values have risen between 10 to 15 percent annually.

As you consider buying a property outside the United States, determine if the currency exchange rates work to your advantage. Understand the differences in financing terms. For example, in Canada, purchasers typically need a down payment of 25 percent, whereas non-Canadians must make a down payment of 25 to 40 percent.

It is always important to understand the covenants under which you may own property in a resort. For example, in Whistler, there are two condominium covenants. The Unrestricted Owner Usage Covenant allows an owner unlimited personal use of his condo, as well as a choice of rental management. The Restricted Owner Usage Covenant offers "revenue pooling" wherein owners are allowed 56 days annually for personal use, with 28 days in the winter season and 28 days in the summer.

OCEAN PROPERTY

Generally, the highest rate of appreciation will be realized for homes closest to the beach. Although there is not much elevation for coastal lots, some lots nevertheless enjoy higher elevations and are situated behind high sand dunes. Such lots are desirable because during rainy seasons and when there is high occupancy of the cottage the septic drain field will have a better chance of functioning than one on a lower lot. Some people foolishly have demolished dunes in order to have a better view of the ocean. This shortsighted effort leaves the dwelling fully exposed to storm water surge damage. Remember, if you can see the ocean, it can *see* you. A wide beach can protect a property by providing more land area to dissipate floodwater plus more area for recreation. Information is available to determine if there is beach erosion, as well as its rate of loss. In some areas, there actually is beach buildup through accretion.

You will want to investigate the cost and availability of storm, flood, and wind insurance. Hire a professional home inspector to check the condition of the property. Also, perform your own detailed inspection. Investigate the likelihood of large future condominium assessments or the prospect of any construction blocking your view of the ocean.

As you peruse ocean resort sales brochures, you will see what initially may seem to be a confusing variety of terms describing the locations of beach properties. You may read some of the following:

Oceanfront. There are no lots between the property and the beach.

Semi-Oceanfront. There is one lot or home between the property and the beach.

Oceanside. There is no major highway between the property and the beach.

Fronts Beach Road. The property is on the opposite side of a road from the beach. Thus, a road must be crossed in order to reach the beach. The number of traffic lanes and volume can affect the appeal of the property.

These same terms may be used to describe the relative location of houses on or near a **sound,** river, or bay.

LAKE PROPERTY

The accessibility of lake frontage property may be impaired by rough terrain as well as the length of the access right of way. Lots situated in rugged terrain may require expensive road construction as well as the expense of acquiring a four-wheel drive vehicle. Also, if a long road leads into the property, a major ongoing maintenance cost may be incurred. Determine what recreational activities are allowed since they can affect the appeal and value of adjacent residences.

Northern Lake Access

Lake accessibility greatly affects the appeal and value of lakefront property. This is especially so in Canada and Alaska and in some northern areas of the United States. It is not widely known, but less than 10 percent of the land in Alaska is privately owned. Most of the "open to entry" staking programs from the state of Alaska allow five acres, which typically measure 330 feet by 660 feet with 330 feet being on the water. Over time, some of these parcels have been subdivided into 2 1/2-acre lots with 165 feet of water frontage. Primary access to water-frontage parcels is by floatplane with the two major considerations being the length of the body of water and its elevation. Most privately owned land is located lower than 3,000 feet in elevation. A major reason for this lot preference is that a floatplane performs far better at sea level than at higher altitudes (Figure 3.1 shows a float plane taking off). A half-mile long lake is sufficient at sea level, but a length of one mile is necessary at 1,000 feet, and a two-mile lake is required at 2,000 feet in altitude.

Another consideration in selecting a property is the topography around the lake. An aircraft must have ample room to climb to a safe altitude during takeoff. A lake surrounded by hills and 200-foot tall spruce trees is far

Figure 3.1
Alaskan floatplane.

more intimidating than a lake with at least a meadow at one end. These differences in access will influence property value. Small lakes often are known as **"Super Cub" lakes,** which implies that it is safe to operate from the lake only with a STOL (short takeoff and landing) aircraft.

Wind direction becomes an issue only for marginal lakes. For best performance, an aircraft should be able to take off into the wind. Wind becomes more of a factor after landing. On large lakes, wind can cause wave action that makes landing and taxiing to a safe mooring nearly impossible. You can expect to pay higher premiums for property located in protected coves and property protected by islands than for wind-exposed land. Sometimes, virtually no market exists for these exposed properties. Thus, a local real estate expert can provide invaluable advice to prospective buyers.

Since most floatplanes are moored in water, the quality of the shoreline is a major issue. An ideal lot has a gently sloping sandy beach that allows the aircraft to taxi to the uplands. Gravel or rocky beaches can damage the bottom of the floats. Also, if the frontage is too steep, the wings and the tail of the aircraft might hit the uplands. At the other extreme, if the water is too shallow, the plane cannot taxi to shore. The market penalizes property with poor aircraft moorage.

Parcels on lakes or rivers with good trout fishing or that provide access to salmon fishing and hunting opportunities are in high demand.

In general, recreational cabins within 50 land miles or 100 air miles of Anchorage or Fairbanks are used year-round. Summer access is via float-planes or perhaps all terrain vehicles (ATVs) or boats. Winter access is restricted to ski planes or snowmobiles. Lakes within 50 miles of a road and relatively accessible by snowmobiles are very popular. Remote properties within 15 to 30 miles of a road tend to command higher prices. In Alaska, when travel time exceeds one hour, property prices begin to decline. Privacy commands a premium. For example, the only privately owned parcel on a lake will sell for significantly more than a similar parcel on comparable nearby lakes that have several privately owned parcels.

As in other areas, premium prices are paid for spectacular views of mountains, glaciers, or water. The crown jewel location in the Anchorage-Fairbanks area is a lot that offers a view of Mt. McKinley.[17]

All-Season Resorts

Resorts with year-round activities can help maximize the number of days of achievable annual rental income. Inquire with local rental agents about the number of days of rental occupancy typical for the area. Further, get an idea of the length of the "shoulder" seasons and other off-peak season rental periods, e.g., Thanksgiving and the spring school break.

Increasingly, people are drawn to mountain ski resorts in the off-season. During these times, the pace is more relaxed, and the summer weather is refreshingly cool compared to temperatures and humidity at lower elevations.

Variety of Activities

Some resorts like to promote themselves as "family resorts." Check carefully to see if the recreational activities will appeal to the entire family. I recall several instances when our teenagers resisted going to our lake cottage because it was "boring." Some resorts build expensive hotels, but conference attendees don't flock there because of limited social activities. Although many resorts have attempted to move toward becoming all-season resorts, some fail to offer both day and evening activities of interest

---

[17] Much of this section was taken from private correspondence to the author from Rick D. Richter, MAI of Richter & Stone, Anchorage, Alaska (June 28, 2003).

to residents and visitors. Generally, they provide daytime activities but offer dining and little else at night. Many people, perhaps you, want to dance, bowl, shop, etc., after dinner and not simply to go back to their hotel room, cottage, or condominium.

The 2002 NAR study of second home buyers indicated that the top three leisure activities chosen by second homeowners in resort areas were beach/lake/water sports (69 percent), hunting/fishing (36 percent), boating (44 percent), winter recreation (21 percent), golf (21 percent), and biking/hiking/horseback riding (16 percent).[18]

---

[18] *The 2002 National Association of REALTORS® Profile of Second-Homeowners*, (Chicago: National Association of REALTORS®, 2003). Used with permission.

4 DETERMINING WHAT YOU NEED

Outlying properties invariably will be less expensive, but there will be less rental demand for them and generally lower price appreciation. You should weigh price against convenience of location and availability of amenities. Most guests at **time-share** units and hotels engage in beach and waterfront activities; snow skiing and golf lag by a wide margin. Water-oriented locations also are favored by vacation homeowners.

You should like the property, and it should serve your needs, which probably will increase the prospects of it fulfilling a subsequent buyer's needs. The following factors should influence your choice of property:

✤ It should excite you.

✤ Buy the best that you can afford.

✤ A cheap property generally stays cheap. It will be hard to sell (unless it has a "knock-out" location and just needs some TLC).

✤ An appealing location and design are always key features.

✦ Check the financial strength of the sponsor/developer. Strong financial strength of the developer for a new home is important in choosing where to buy a home.

✦ Track the price history, i.e., appreciation, of the specific property and of neighboring houses.

Is it reasonable to believe that the recent appreciation rate can be sustained? Between 2000 and 2003, many homes at North Carolina's Outer Banks enjoyed 20 to 30 percent annual price increases. This rapid price run-up created strong demand for vacation housing and prompted strong construction activity and an oversupply of homes, which likely will result in slower price increases in the near term. You should consider whether a vacation property likely will appreciate sufficiently since you have alternative uses for your money—ranging from other real estate investments to securities or buying less costly **fractional ownership** shares or renting with the earnings from other investments. The two basic sources of return on a real estate investment are rent and appreciation. As a rule, the rental income will not cover the mortgage debt service and other operating expenses such as real estate taxes, rent commissions, insurance, repairs and maintenance, and public utilities. A few years ago, vacation property owners may have earned 10 percent on the value of their properties (before operating expenses). Today, a 5 percent return (gross rent/purchase price) is probably more realistic. Appreciation is essential to a successful vacation property's financial success and often is the major component of profit. One couple bought a Mid-Atlantic creek-front retirement home in 1999 and thought that they had overpaid at that time. Five years later, they sold it to a West Coast couple—realizing a 24 percent annual increase in value. This profit outperformed the rest of their investment portfolio by a wide margin.

PRESENT AND FUTURE APPEAL

In searching for a place to vacation or even retire, you are best served if you can find a locale where year-round activities are available. It will be easier to rent and eventually sell your property in such an area. Also, a longer tourist season translates into a longer rental season plus greater

Figure 4.1
Bachelor Gulch ski area with Sawatch Mountain Range in background.

demand when you are ready to sell. If there are more base village activities at the ski resort, there obviously will be more engaging activities for both skiers and nonskiers, including off-peak season activities such as hiking, biking, swimming, and canoeing. Determine what evening activities are available for your family and guests. Many people expect a variety of restaurants, dancing, and entertainment venues. C. J. Julin, sales and marketing director for Copper Mountain's resort development projects, stated, "We're no longer in the ski industry, we're in the mountain entertainment industry. It's more than just going up and making a couple of turns."[19] (Figure 4.1 depicts a Colorado ski resort winter scene.)

If you are, or soon will become, a mature vacation homeowner, you probably will want a separate study for your computer and related supplies. This room should have adequate natural and artificial lighting, telephone lines, and wiring. Check on the ease and cost of cable hookup for your Internet connection. Seniors log onto the Internet more than any other age group whether for communicating with relatives and friends or

---

[19] Robert Christie Mill, *Resorts—Management and Operation* (New York: John Wiley & Sons, Inc., 2001), p. 429.

monitoring investments. A room suitable for exercise equipment may be attractive as well.

Definitely scrutinize the condition of the home. Sometimes, a few homes will be renovated in a neighborhood and sell for a higher than usual price. The property that you are viewing may be priced as if it has been renovated, which, of course, is too high.

Kitchen and bathroom renovations can make a home considerably more appealing and warrant higher prices. Updated appliances and cosmetic improvements, such as interior painting and carpet replacement, also deserve higher prices. You should expect a clean, bright, and up-to-date interior. Observe the typical ratio of full bathrooms to bedrooms. In many areas, there may be one fewer baths than bedrooms. For example, a four-bedroom home would have three baths. I once considered an attractive oceanside cottage with six bedrooms served by only two full and two half-baths. This underserved house initially was a questionable purchase until I saw a way to economically expand a ground-level half-bath into a full bath. This simple modification created a private two-bedroom suite.

In some parts of the country, some government incentives are intended to encourage senior residents to relocate. For example, Florida has a homestead exemption. This means that a permanent resident of Florida may reduce his or her real estate assessed value by $25,000, thus reducing the annual real estate tax bill. This provides another benefit in that a retiree's home, having a homestead, is generally exempt from a forced sale by his creditors. Rental property, however, does not qualify for this homestead benefit. In 2003, Summit County, Colorado, commenced a property tax exemption for persons who are 65 years old and have owned and occupied the same Summit County primary residence for at least 10 consecutive years. Qualified residents have 50 percent of the first $200,000 of their residence exempted from property taxes.

Often, an ocean cottage or mountain or lake cabin provides an emotional anchor for a family. We rarely remain in the same community throughout our work careers so it becomes particularly appealing when a family can visit the vacation place where they, their parents, and their children spent many enjoyable days and nights in the past. A vacation place can provide a place to gather siblings and children and grandparents and grandchildren for peaceful visits and to relive and add to wonderful memories.

Key Retirement Issues

A 1997 survey by *Where to Retire* magazine identified the following as the most important determinants in searching for a resort-oriented retirement location:

✤ Low crime rate

✤ Good hospitals nearby

✤ Low overall cost of living

✤ Mild climate

✤ Low overall taxes

✤ Low housing costs

✤ Friendly neighbors

✤ Major city nearby

✤ No state income tax

✤ Active social and cultural environment

Resorts and retirement communities have a greater chance of succeeding if they are located within 30 minutes of medical services and no more than one hour from a municipal airport. Other amenities that today's retirees seek include upscale services such as gardening areas, nature trails, fully equipped physical fitness centers with trainers, and connectivity to high-speed Internet service. They expect high-quality construction and larger rooms. Expected, too, is the ability to socialize with different age groups and not just people of their age.

Another important group of investors is the pre-retirees who want a balance of recreational activities, culture, and an opportunity to remain engaged professionally on a part-time basis.

Accessibility of Resort

Most prospective vacation homeowners choose a property either in the same state (42 percent) or in the same region (19 percent). The median distance from their primary home is 185 miles, yet one-fourth of vacation homes are more than 1,000 miles from home. For trips under 1,500 miles, over three-quarters of vacation homeowners travel by car. For the entire United States, 61 percent of vacation homes were reported to be in a resort/recreation area, with 21 percent being in rural areas.[20]

CULTURAL, ENTERTAINMENT, AND EDUCATIONAL OPPORTUNITIES

If you want to upgrade your job skills, expand your knowledge of the arts, or perhaps begin a part-time career in a different field after retirement, find out what educational opportunities are available in or near the resort. You may want to periodically take short courses or continuing education courses in areas that you were too busy to study during your career.

From the perspective of you and your family, as well as personal and rental guests, satisfaction will be greatest when the resort provides choices among a variety of activities, including downhill skiing, snow boarding, cross-country skiing, snow shoeing, tubing, ice skating, spa, dancing, concerts, horseback riding, indoor and outdoor swimming, kayaking, rafting and canoeing, fishing, hiking, jogging, biking, golfing, and tennis. Also, guests will enjoy educational opportunities involving nature and local history, opportunities for personal growth, and a variety of dining venues. Today's retirees are looking for something more than a country club environment. They want to be situated in an intellectually stimulating environment where there are adventure, fitness programs, and enjoyable social activities.

CREATE A CHECKLIST OF PREFERENCES

Resort home buyers typically are buying a lifestyle, such as semiretirement where they can get away from worldly pressures, use modern communications technology, stroll through an inviting environment of scenic coasts or mountains, ski or swim for a while, and then go back to work without having left their neighborhood.

In selecting a property, you will want to talk to REALTORS®, read sales ads in the local paper, and read local real estate magazines. These should include both for-sale and rental publications so you can get an idea of pricing and rental rates. After studying this information, you can then

---

[20] *The 2002 National Association of REALTORS® Profile of Second-Homeowners* (Chicago: National Association of REALTORS®, 2003). Used with permission.

refine your initial criteria by adjusting your vacation property needs to fit the prices of homes that are currently available.

Try to use the Internet as much as possible, especially to take virtual house tours. From your home, you can begin to classify available vacation properties by location, design, size, and amenities in various price brackets. Locate computer-literate sales agents who can provide you with information to assist in your sales search. Perhaps they can also assist you in finding a place to rent on your visits to the resort. You will want to have visited and stayed several times at different seasons as you refine your purchase search. I have identified prospective properties through local Multiple Listing Services (MLS) and on individual REALTOR® companies' Web sites. After the agents had screened my preliminary selections and added others, they better understood what I was seeking. My visits in search of a vacation property were considerably more productive than simply showing up and then trying to sort through prospective properties.

According to a 2002 national survey, the two primary reasons for buying a second home are (1) personal/family retreat and (2) vacations. Somewhat fewer people purchase second homes to serve as a primary residence after retirement, to diversify their investments, or to receive rental income.[21] This survey further revealed that among persons not presently owning a second home, most wanted to be near an ocean, river, or lake (47 percent), 21 percent wanted to be close to the mountains and natural attractions, 10 percent wanted good investment potential, and 8 percent wanted to be close to a preferred vacation area.[22]

The check list in Figure 4.2 brings some order to the several and often confusing factors that you might consider when deciding which property best meets your ownership criteria.

DISTINGUISH BETWEEN YOUR WANTS AND NEEDS

Initially, you may think that you must have an oceanfront cottage. As you weigh the cost of this choice, prioritize your needs. You may find that you will be satisfied by either purchasing an oceanfront or oceanview condominium or a detached home within a five-minute walk from

---

[21] *The 2002 National Association of REALTORS® Profile of Second-Homeowners* (Chicago: National Association of REALTORS®, 2003). Used with permission.
[22] Ibid.

Figure 4.2   Check List of Ownership Criteria

Amenity	Important to Have	Makes Little or No Difference
Rustic rural area		
Upbeat urban area		
Snow skiing/snow boarding		
Hiking		
Water sports and fishing		
Ocean, river, or lake		
Variety of golf courses		
Entertainment/shows/dancing		
Cultural activities		
Good health care		
Moderate year-round climate		
Change of seasons		
Variety of shopping opportunities		
Minimal ownership responsibilities		
Within a three-hour automobile drive		

the beach. Decide which is more important—a prime location and lesser home or a nicer home and a less appealing location.

VACATIONING IN-SEASON AND OFF-SEASON SAMPLING

Make it a point to visit the resort area both during the peak season and the off-season. You may find that the climate does not suit you in one of the seasons. That may be the peak tourist season when you could rent the property. Some prospective owners find the traffic and crowd hassles during the high or busy season are unappealing. One couple purchased a cottage on North Carolina's Outer Banks and later discovered that it was a grueling task to leave their property to play golf on summer weekends. It required almost as much time to drive their car to and from the off-island golf courses as they actually spent on the courses. They coped with the traffic by staying at their vacation home on weekends and playing golf during the week when it was less crowded and cheaper.

Others have visited a resort during the high season and loved the temperatures and many activities and variety of shops only to discover that the off-season was not as appealing, convenient, or enjoyable as they had expected. Others absolutely love the idea of avoiding the high season crowds and relish the tranquility of the off-seasons. By visiting your property during the off-season, you can rent it to others. These peak season rentals can substantially offset your mortgage payments and related housing expenses.

Ideally, you should stay during different seasons if you plan to retire in a particular community. Learn to view it through the eyes of year-round residents as well as learn whether there is too much congestion and noise during the peak season. Will you enjoy living there if your next-door neighbors change every week? Also, how do you react to the seasonal changes in weather and insects? Are there adequate services and shopping available during the off-season?

Now Do You Still *Really* Want to Live Here?

Your decision to purchase a vacation property may be influenced by when and how much you and your family intend to use it. For example, you may want to use it seasonally, for two-week vacations, or as a transition to your primary retirement home. If part of your motivation for buying a vacation home is to hold it while you plan for retirement, you may use the same check list mentioned earlier in this chapter, but you probably will weight some of the features differently than if you were buying only for vacation usage. If you plan to eventually use the property for retirement, then think now about what amenities you will want in both the community and dwelling. For example, you may want the house to include a master bedroom suite, upgraded telecommunications wiring, and a one-floor house plan. (This topic is developed in more detail in Chapter 6.)

Some major concerns in choosing a vacation community are affordability of the locale, including cost of living and the various local and state taxes. You will certainly want to evaluate the cultural amenities, continuing learning opportunities, outdoor recreational facilities, health care facilities, and weather conditions. Is the season when you wish to use the property oppressively hot and humid or unbearably cold and snowy? Ideally, the weather is moderate for each of the four seasons. Another factor to consider is the scale of the area. Do you prefer a large, busy, but comprehensive resort or more of a small-town environment, but with fewer conveniences?

In the 1990s, many retirees stressed affordable housing, and in turn they sought small condominiums. But today's retirees seek resort-style communities with fitness centers, high capacity home telecommunications wiring, golf, tennis, jogging paths and hiking trails, swimming, as well as self-improvement opportunities. They are more active at their age than were their parents and look at retirement as a process rather than the end of employment. It seems that R&R (rest and relaxation) has been the mantra of vacationers forever. Today's vacationer is probably more interested in education, enrichment, and entertainment than was the case just a few years ago.

It may be a mistake to limit your housing search just to age-restricted communities. Marshall Ames, vice president of Lennar, a large Miami-based homebuilding firm active in the seniors market, says, "We have found that the age-restricted label has become a stigma, and even the term 'active adult' turns some people off. We now call them private resort communities. Other research shows that property values tend to appreciate more quickly in a non-age-restricted community where owners can sell to a wider range of buyers. . . ."[23]

A fundamental rule for vacation property owners is: "If you can't reach it, you can't rent it or sell it (profitably)." Similarly, you won't enjoy a vacation property that is so remote that it takes a major effort for you to reach on weekends or for holidays. Generally, it is preferable if you can find a property in a community where the zoning code restricts haphazard strip commercial development or mobile homes from being mixed in with detached single-family homes. Also, you will most likely realize greater future value enhancement where there is little vacant land available for competitive developments, which tilts the supply-demand equation in your favor.

---

[23] Lewis M. Goodkin, "Retirement," *Urban Land* (April 2000), p. 76.

The appeal and reputation varies significantly from town to town, especially for coastal resort communities. You want to buy in a community that enjoys a good reputation and is sought out by buyers and renters. A simple purchase strategy is to buy where people want to visit and live.

5 | REFINING YOUR SEARCH (WHAT TO LOOK FOR)

In this chapter, we discuss different ways to identify prospective properties that you may want to consider for purchase and where and when you may discover bargains. The merits of setting your own course and not following the buying cycles of the majority and how off-season buying may offer good deals are covered. Later, advice is provided on buying foreclosed properties, and pointers are given on why some properties are worth more than others.

SOURCES OF LEADS

Try to subscribe to a local real estate sales publication. These may be published monthly or quarterly. Use a search engine on your computer's Internet service to locate a local REALTOR'S®'s office Web site. This source, in addition to classified ads in the local newspaper, will keep you up to date on price trends for different types and locations of property. Retain these materials so that later you can compare the described properties to their sale prices. This sales information often is available from municipal government Web sites. Another valuable form of information that may be published in the newspaper is a periodic listing of community association liens filed against property owners. The existence of a lien suggests an owner's disinterest in his vacation property or financial difficulties. Spend some time in the local assessor's office or commissioner of revenue's office to learn the address of out-of-area property owners.

View properties (either lots or improved properties) that are of interest to you. Some of these may appear to have been unvisited for a number of months by the owners. Possibly, the property was bought for the family's use and the children have grown up and are no longer interested in visiting the home. The owners may have been transferred to another job in a more distant state. They may have purchased the property with grand visions of renting it extensively to offset much of their mortgage debt service and real estate taxes, etc., but the property's rental performance may have been disappointing. Contact these people to determine whether they have an interest in selling their property. You should have a fairly clear idea of how much you will pay for it. Ask for permission to inspect the property before making an offer. If you make an offer, remind the owner that he will save paying a real estate agent's commission by selling directly to you.

Some resort communities built 20 to 30 years ago appealed to retirees then. Now, many of those communities have residents who are in their '80s. With limited appeal today, these properties may be priced below their market value. They can be picked up from estates or as the residents move to nursing homes or hospitals.

Another source is resort properties offered for sale by the owner (FSBO, sometimes called Fizzbo). Such sellers are motivated to omit a **real estate broker** from the selling process because they are experienced sellers, think they are experienced, or want to make a sale without paying a sales commission. Without the presence of a broker to temper the owner's initial offering price, you may find the property either under- or overpriced. If underpriced, be prepared to move quickly (being certain to include the appropriate protective clauses in the purchase contract) because the property likely won't stay on the market very long. Further, don't expect to benefit by reducing the price by the full amount of the omitted real estate commission. The seller has his eye on this savings as well, so you might reasonably expect to split the difference or maybe reduce the price by approximately 3 percent in addition to however much you hope the seller will come off the asking price. On the other hand, if the property is overpriced, you may not want to invest too much time in pursuing a purchase unless it has been on the market for a long time.

Two other things should be remembered when dealing with a seller directly. First, you have lost the negotiating buffer provided by a real estate agent. Therefore, you will need to be more diplomatic in dealing with the property owner who probably is more "thin skinned" than a seasoned real estate professional and may be emotionally attached to the property. Second, do not allow the seller to hold the deposit on the property. Keep it in escrow with a third party, such as the closing attorney or with a title insurance company.

Are There Any Bargains Left?

You should be thinking of the future resale prospects when you consider buying a vacation property. In any market, it usually is a mistake to either buy a cheaply built or poorly located home. Check to determine how long a "cheap" property has been listed. Even at a below-market price, it still may be overpriced and remain cheap later when you attempt to sell it. Thus, approach such a property with as much caution as you would a poisonous snake. A so-called "handyman special" may be beyond saving. For example, it may cost you $100,000 to buy plus another $200,000 to restore and then it would only be worth $180,000.

In a rising market, it can be a mistake to wait until you can "afford" to buy. As a wealthy real estate investor once said to the author, somewhat in jest, "Do you remember that property that you didn't buy last year? You should have!" This does not mean to willy-nilly rush to buy a property; always deliberately and unemotionally evaluate any prospective property purchase even though you really are excited about the prospect of owning it. Rising prices may make vacation properties less and less affordable with the passage of time. Property values may be rising faster than you can save to purchase one. Many disappointed prospective vacation property owners have waited until they thought they could comfortably afford a home only to discover that they had fallen farther behind. Thus, one strategy is to buy a lot now and build later. The greatest part of the appreciation of a property is realized by the underlying lot, which may represent 30 to 60 percent of the total vacation property's value. This strategy can cut in half the initial outlay for a future home while you enjoy the benefits of an appreciating asset.

Figure 5.1
Modest, but
attractive, cottage.

Courtesy of Seaside Vacations, Kitty Hawk, North Carolina.

A key to finding a bargain is to carefully assess the condition of the property, its neighborhood, and the state of the local real estate market. Further, consider how much you may have to invest in the property in order to have an appealing property for renters, subsequent buyers, and, of course, your family. Finally, is there an ample profit margin left in the deal to justify your purchasing the property at the listing price?

Before committing yourself to buying a property, get estimates from reliable contractors in order to determine how much it will cost to make the property structurally sound and attractive. (Figure 5.1 shows a fairly ordinary cottage that, if well located to amenities, can be a good investment.) If the acquisition cost plus renovation costs leave you with no profit margin, then walk away from this candidate property. Even if you plan to use the property for personal use, you cannot afford to overpay. Remember, a large part of the profit is made when you buy a property. Generally, you can remake most properties to increase their appeal and marketability, but you can *never, never* overcome an unappealing, remote, or inaccessible neighborhood. Location is one of the three most important factors in successful real estate purchases. The other two are timing of purchase (and sale) and skilled management while you own it.

Buying a sound, attractive, well-designed and constructed property in a rising market certainly can be thought of as a bargain. Walt Molony of the National Association of REALTORS® states, "oceanfront property in the Mid-Atlantic region doubled in value between 1997 and 2001."[24]

---

[24] Broderick Perkins, "Second-Home Sales Eased But Prices Jumped in 2001, NAR Reports" (June 3, 2002), *Profile of Home Buyers and Sellers* by the National Association of Realtors.

Remember to ask questions and keenly observe which neighborhoods and locations are outperforming the overall local rental and sales market.

You Are Not Obliged to Follow the Crowd

We all are influenced by the "herd instinct." That is, we tend to buy when everyone else is buying; likewise, we sell when the common instinct of others is to sell. It takes courage to go against predominant buying and selling trends. Yet, the very best time to buy real estate is when a particular class of property, such as vacation homes, is out of vogue. The best buys can be realized when the masses adhere to conventional wisdom and are selling. As legendary investment figure John Templeton has said many times, "The greatest bargains can only be found at the point of maximum pessimism." To win on both ends of an investment, you should consider buying in a down or buyers' market when supply exceeds demand and you have a number of choices at comparatively favorable prices. You should sell when prices are elevated and there are more buyers than properties available for sale. The latter market phase is also known as a "sellers' market." In such markets, I have seen agents receiving multiple offers on the same property within several hours. It is almost like an auction where the seller has the luxury of sorting through several offers—some in excess of the offering price.

You may find that the property that fits your needs and pocketbook is either in a strong location, but in need of some TLC, or perhaps it is just a little off the beaten path and is a structurally sound and architecturally appealing property. Either situation may present an opportunistic purchase.

Off-Season Purchase

Explore the prospect of buying a vacation property in the off-season. You may be able to obtain a property for less than during the spring and summer for beach property and in the fall and winter for mountain ski resort property. There will be fewer prospective buyers for either type of vacation property in the off-season. Competition will have decreased for all properties. Also, the owner may be getting anxious to sell quickly since the property failed to sell in the peak demand season. By checking offerings from the past season, you may find some properties whose listing agreements have expired. Almost automatically, you will be able to reduce the sales price by part of the real estate commission that the seller otherwise would have paid. Just be certain that the expired listing is not a property that was shown to you earlier by a real estate agent. She may still be legally entitled to a commission since she was the "procuring cause" for the purchase.

To some extent, a seller will discount the price by the amount of his carrying cost until the beginning of the next prime rental season. Keep in mind that you have merely changed positions with the seller, even though you have received a slightly lower price. Now, it is your turn to carry the property until the next peak rental season. The trade-off probably is a smaller selection of properties in the off-season versus more highly motivated sellers.

Foreclosure Sales

It is possible to buy resort property at mortgage foreclosure sales. A good starting point is to subscribe to the local newspaper where foreclosure auctions are advertised. To broaden the scope of your search, you may be able to connect with someone in the mortgage department of a bank that is active in a particular resort market. If so, inquire about repossessed properties, which are also known as REO (real estate owned) properties that banks want to move out of their inventories. A search of Internet mortgage sites serving your specific market may also be productive.

The winning bid should cover payment of real estate taxes in arrears, unpaid mortgage interest, and legal fees including the substitute trustee's fee. In a nonjudicial sale, this amount may be announced by the substitute trustee, or it will be the opening bid by this person. This amount will cover all of the debt owed to the lender. Several things will require caution in this area. Just because a property is scheduled to be auctioned does not mean that it will actually be sold. I have found that no more than 10 to 20 percent of advertised properties are actually sold at auction. Most owners in default will find the means to bring their account up to date, or the lender may restructure the loan to assist the borrower with his payments. It is wise to call the substitute trustee (generally a law firm selling the property) the day before it is scheduled to be auctioned to determine its status. Identify the property by location, date of sale, and file number. Part of the problem that you face is even if the auction goes forth, you will have very little time to obtain a cashier's check and get to the auction. If it is as much as four hours away from your home city, you will have lost an entire day from work. Plus, you may not be able to justify a bid price that will allow you to acquire the property and still earn an adequate profit margin. As part of the prebidding process, you should compile sales records from the newspaper on recent sales of similar properties. Understand the property as best you can, which may be limited to an exterior inspection prior to the day of the auction. Some auctions take place on the premises where you can inspect the property an hour or so prior to the auction. Others occur in front of the local courthouse, where you cannot inspect the interior. The lack of an interior inspection may not matter in some cases, but without it, you truly are buying an unknown quantity. I have seen houses stripped of electrical fixtures, mirrors, and generally trashed prior to a foreclosure sale. Also, if you want to upgrade the heating system to include air conditioning, you should know if it has a forced warm air system or an electrical baseboard heat system. The latter does not have the ducts required for installation of central air conditioning.

Keep in mind that you may not actually see the property until the day of the auction, assuming you make an exterior inspection en route to the auction, which will likely be in front of the courthouse. Another point to remember is that you will need to have ample cash to pay the entire auction price (which will probably include payment of real estate taxes and mortgage payments that are in arrears, plus penalties) and a substitute trustee fee within perhaps two weeks. Having a **line of credit** is one source of ready cash for such purchases.

Why Are Some Properties More Valuable than Others?

Prices of improved properties may vary because of such factors as the following:

1. Age and condition: A newer vacation property will require fewer repairs and entail lower maintenance costs.

2. A house with modern appliances and a functional floor plan will be popular and, in turn, command a comparatively high price.

3. An appealing design will draw more prospective buyers and attract higher prices than homes with a less appealing design.

4. A prime location will bring maximum traffic and attract the highest prices.

For both vacant lots and improved properties, the following observations will be helpful in identifying key location influences on value. These price patterns are based on several surveys and observations of water-oriented resorts as reported in the author's book *Land Valuation Adjustment Procedures and Assignments*: A study of 297 residential lot sales on the Atlantic barrier island of Seabrook south of Charleston, South Carolina, found that ocean views added 147 percent to lot values while lots on creeks or marshes added 115 percent, and golf course lot locations added 39 percent to lot prices.

A survey of 18 coastal golf communities by Ravenel, Inc., of Kiawah Island, South Carolina, showed that compared to interior lots, the prices progressed upward from lagoon, fairway, fairway/lagoon, marsh, deep-water, and ultimately oceanfront lots. The premiums paid for the lots above interior lots were as follows: lagoon (+155%), fairway (+160%), fairway/lagoon (+240%), marsh (+260%), and deepwater (+715%). The deepwater lots had sufficient water depth to accommodate a pier for deep draft boats such as sail and shrimp boats. Oceanfront lots brought a premium of 175 percent over the average price paid for the deepwater lots. In many instances, oceanfront lots have become so valuable that they bring prices above $1 million; sometimes, existing cottages are torn down to make way for larger, more expensive houses.

An example of the different values of water-oriented residential lots is shown in the following example:

High Lot on a Point	Good Water Depth & view	Waterfront, with Limited View	Off-Water Lots
$200,000	$150,000	$100,000	$25,000

Several factors influence the popularity and value of waterfront properties. Generally, a higher elevation lot with a gentle slope to the water is superior to a low-lying lot that will be susceptible to storm-water surges in hurricanes and tropical storms. Also, a higher lot is less likely to have toilets on a septic system fail due to high water levels. A gently sloping lot with a low bank at the water line will typically be more usable and not require expensive stone rip rap or a wooden bulkhead.

The direction of prevailing winds, especially winter storms, can affect property values. Be careful to determine this direction since lots that are protected from these winds sell for more than similar lots on the opposite exposed shore.

Check water impoundment lakes for the variation between high and low water levels. If it varies more than two or three feet, floating docks with steep steps may pose problems.

In tidal waters, look for choke points where passage into and out of creeks is difficult because the water level is less than three feet, which limits the sale of the property to prospects who own small, shallow draft boats. Lot values will be impaired if a lot is on the shore away from the channel. Mud flats and shallow water may lie between the property and the channel. You can detect this to some extent by studying a marine chart. Better yet, inspect a waterfront lot from a boat with either a depth sounder or make up a pole with foot markers on it so you can accurately measure the water depth at low tide at several key points in front of the property.

Low bridges between a property and the mouth of a river or creek can adversely affect its value. For example, in the Jupiter/Tequesta area of Florida, waterfront lots on the Loxahatchee River upriver from a fixed bridge are worth as much as 40 percent less than lots downriver from the bridge.

People often generalize when they refer to "view lots." As you will see in the following illustration, mountain resort lot (and home) prices vary depending on the views provided by the properties. These mountain view lots are ranked from least to most desirable:

- ✤ *Interior.* An interior lot may offer some attractions, such as scenic trees and terrain, as well as proximity to resort amenities, such as tennis courts, ski slopes, and exercise facilities.

- ✤ *Stream.* These views may be seasonal depending on tree foliage. In the summer, it may dry up. Its appeal also increases if it is a year-round fishing stream.

- ✤ *Golf fairway or greens views.* This view is appealing since it visually extends the expanse and depth of a lot through additional green space that the property owner does not have to maintain.

- ✤ *Lake.* Depending on the lake size and scenery, this category may be higher ranked. Larger size lakes allow sailing, but the congestion from noisy motor boating and jet skiing can become a nuisance to lakefront property owners.

✤ *Narrow or short-distance views.* These views are limited and frequently narrow and sometimes are called "keyhole" view lots.

✤ *Sunset views.* Many purchasers prefer the restful serenity of these views at day's end.

✤ *Distant views.* These views are found along mountain ledges and on elevated lots where the vistas may be uninterrupted for many miles.[25]

Some properties are more expensive than others for a number of reasons. Coastal and waterfront properties may be in a flood zone. Some of these are eligible for federal flood insurance, some require more expensive private insurance, and still others may not qualify for flood insurance at all.

Sometimes, single-family homes are favored over condominiums. At other times, condominiums may be more popular because they offer better access to public shuttle service or are near amenities such as ski slopes or the waterfront. Also, single-family detached homes may have become so expensive that demand shifts to less expensive condominiums. A municipal building moratorium may be imposed for such reasons as growth having outpaced the availability of public utilities. In such cases, demand for undeveloped land may suffer, while improved lots (lots with homes on them) may bring a premium due to their relative scarcity.

Look for a resort that is technologically advanced where you can work and relax without having to break up your visits by returning home to communicate with the staff or clients. Previous rigid lines between leisure and work time have become increasingly blurred.

Is Renting to Others Prohibited?

You may plan to use the property for personal use plus rent it to others when you are not using it. If so, very early in your search, you will want to check the subdivision **restrictive covenants** or condominium regime

---

[25] Much of the material from this section is taken from the author's book, *Land Valuation Adjustment Procedures and Assignments* (Appraisal Institute: Chicago, 2001), Chapter 14, "Location Adjustments for Resort Lots," and Chapter 18, "Residential Waterfront Property."

documents to determine any rental restrictions. For example, you may be prohibited from leasing over a certain number of times annually, limited to leasing for six months at a time, or not allowed to rent to parties who have pets. The first two restrictions could upset your desire to rent the home and offset part of your mortgage, insurance, taxes, and other related ownership costs.

6 | WHAT TYPE OF HOME YOU SHOULD BUY

Once you have decided on the state and locale in which you desire to own your vacation property, you should next determine the type of house that best satisfies your needs. A very critical step in this selection process is obtaining a home inspection. You want to be certain there will be no expensive repair costs after the home has been purchased. Buying either a previously owned or a newly constructed home both have advantages.

One buying strategy is to buy at the preconstruction stage to achieve a lower price and wider choice of floor plans. Choices are also available between detached and attached homes as well as between exclusive ownership and upkeep of the entire property or shared ownership with accompanying professional maintenance of the building's exterior, landscaping, and recreation facilities.

HOME INSPECTION

You must obtain a home inspection! This is no place to be "penny wise." You may save $300 or $400 and easily risk spending 10 times that amount on costly undetected structural repairs or fail to discover a potential fire hazard. You may choose not to use an inspection firm recommended by the real estate agent. Avoid using anyone known for "going along to make the deal." If the inspector is not state licensed, it would be wise to determine if he is a member of the American Society of Home Inspectors. To determine this or even to locate a member in your locale, either call (800) 743–2744 or go to *http://www.ashi.org*. Alternatively, you may want to use electrical, plumbing, and carpentry trades people and a good HVAC technician and termite inspector. Certainly use one or more of these specialists if you suspect that there is a problem with one of the building components or systems and you want to get an estimate of its repair or replacement. If repairs are necessary, require copies of the invoices showing the work has been performed (at seller's expense) and require that the inspector approve the work before you buy the property.

If you suspect there may be some substantial structural, HVAC, electrical, or plumbing problem, you definitely will want to retain a home inspector. The same applies to buying a home where the seller has made the sale on an *as-is basis*. In this case, insist more than ever that the seller disclose all visible and hidden property defects and note the same in the sales contract.

Make the purchase contingent on an acceptable *whole house* inspection report so that you can be relieved from buying a defective house. The seller may pay to repair the identified deficiencies, or you can cancel the contract without penalty. Knowing the cost of repairs can be useful in negotiating the purchase price as well. Some deficiencies, such as a deteriorating neighborhood, foundation deficiencies or damage, inferior design qualities, or severe shoreline erosion, may be "deal breakers" that you should walk away from before signing a purchase contract. Other property flaws, such as worn-out or outdated carpeting, bath and electrical fixtures, or a roof in need of replacement, may be negotiating points. If you are able to gain price concessions that will allow you to stay within your predetermined price plus renovation costs, then you should go forward with the purchase.

The value of a home inspector is maximized by clearly specifying (preferably in writing) the key points on which you expect the inspector to report. Even if you do not identify these areas of concern, review with the inspector upon completion of his inspection the following:

- *Foundation* for structural soundness and waterproofing. Look for cracks and signs of settling as well as dampness in the crawl space.

- *Exterior walls and roof,* checking for leaks and shingles that may need to be replaced soon and walls that soon may need repairs or painting. Inspect fiberboard siding and Dryvit for deterioration and rot.

- *Drainage,* including gutters and down spouts; checking to determine if they are clogged or have ample pitch for water to run off. See if there is rotten fascia board behind the gutters. Does the ground slope away from the house so that rainwater is carried away from the foundation? Is the basement dry?

- *Plumbing* for leaks and whether there is sufficient water pressure (turn on bathroom faucets and simultaneously flush toilet); check to see if water heater is of adequate size and meets the building code.

- *Heating/air conditioning system;* is it modern and energy efficient?

- *Electrical system;* is circuit breaker of adequate capacity, are there sufficient outlets, and are they in working order?

- *Windows and doors;* are there signs of dry rot, broken panes, or thermopane seals failure; do all doors and windows open and close satisfactorily? Some painters will leave windows stuck in a closed position.

- *Interior floors, walls, and ceilings* should be free of stains (indication of water leaks or pets not being house broken). If floors are stained, adjust your offer by the amount to refinish them. Check floors around showers, tubs, toilets, and radiators for rotted wood.

- *Kitchen appliances;* are they in sound condition, and if freestanding, do they convey with the property?

- *Adequacy of insulation* in walls and ceiling, including under the ground floor. If there is an attic fan, does it function, and does it operate automatically?

- *Well and individual septic systems;* is the well sufficiently deep to produce a reliable supply of water during the dry seasons? Have the water tested by the local or state health department. Are the septic drain fields and pump working properly?

✦ Test the property for presence of *radon, asbestos ceiling and floor tiles and insulation, and lead paint.*

✦ *Condition and appeal of driveway, walks, fencing, and landscaping.*

Make every effort to be present when the inspection is made, possibly when you are compiling an inventory of personal property that is to transfer with the real estate. If the seller is not present during your preparation of the inventory list, she should receive a copy promptly so that she can indicate her concurrence in writing. Also, the inspector may expect to be paid once the inspection has been made. Your presence and payment reaffirm that you are the client.

He can point out costly problems for you or items that simply may need attention soon. The inspector may be able to give an estimate of the cost of making any repairs. This may influence your decision to proceed with the purchase or encourage you to ask the seller to pay repair costs, especially if there is a major structural problem or replacement needed, such as water heater, heat and air conditioning unit(s), or roofing. You may have some specific areas you want to have checked out. I have found they can provide good advice concerning maintenance practices and identify equipment or systems that may need attention, such as HVAC systems that are over 15–20 years old. Additionally, they are a good source of names for HVAC maintenance companies and other repair/service contractors.

Existing or New Home?

One factor to account for in setting an offering price for a resort home is the physical condition of the property. A property that has been in a rental plan probably will have experienced greater wear than one used only by the owners. Greater wear equates to a larger initial expenditure for replacement of furnishings (if included in the sale) as well as possible larger repairs to the dwelling's structural components.

New Homes

New homes may be better insulated and have modern kitchens, heating/air conditioning, and electrical systems. Consequently, the cost of operating a newer home should be less than what it would be for an older home. The

Figure 6.1
Outer Banks
cottage.

Courtesy of Seaside Vacations, Kitty Hawk, North Carolina.

same applies to repairs. The chance of hidden flaws in a new home is less, but these construction and design flaws may not appear for a year or so. You may, if you are willing to pay the added cost, purchase a home built to your specifications. Be careful, however, not to make the design features too individualistic or you may have great trouble selling the house later. Most likely, a typical buyer will discount the price by the amount to replace any peculiar features. Another important attraction of new homes is that they tend to increase in value faster than older homes (Figure 6.1 is illustrative of a modern beach cottage).

Partially offsetting these advantages are the sometimes monotonous appearance of newly developed subdivisions with look-alike homes and minimal landscaping. The quality of labor may be inferior to that found in older homes, but over the years, building codes have become more stringent—resulting in better-designed homes. Interior trim and hardware are often comparatively modest in new homes. A new dwelling, if served by an individual septic system, probably will enjoy a longer period before the absorptive capacity of the drain field fails.

In addition to local sources, the National Association of Homebuilders **(http://www.homebuilder.com)** identifies listings on newly built homes by community. Both new and previously owned home listings are available, including pictures and virtual tours at **http://www.realtor.com**.

PRECONSTRUCTION RESERVATION

Reserving a property, often a resort condominium, prior to its construction offers another possibility for acquiring a vacation property. Developers generally need to presell a certain number of units in order to secure development/construction financing. Therefore, they are motivated to offer a financial incentive to prospective buyers in order to secure this funding at the earliest possible date. Pricing for a residential unit typically advances as the developer progresses through successive stages of construction. There-fore, the least costly and widest array of choices of units is available prior to construction. A disadvantage of buying property in this way is the inabi-lity to actually inspect prospective residences.

Basically, the way this program works is for a prospect to make a mod-est payment to reserve the opportunity to purchase a particular property at a future date. By depositing, for example, $5,000 in escrow, a buyer can reserve the right to purchase the property at a future date. Perhaps six months later, the prospective buyer must either cancel his reservation or invest additional capital. Then, maybe in another year when the project is completed, the buyer must close on the purchase of the property with a 20 to 25 percent down payment.

In using this method, the buyer is "betting" the value of his property will have risen during the period between signing the reservation and advancing the full down payment at closing. You can control a sizeable investment for a relatively modest sum of money.

An example of this acquisition method follows: one-bedroom ocean-front with a reservation price of $189,950; deposit, $5,000; initial down payment, $19,000; balance of down payment, $19,000; loan amount, $151,900. The estimated monthly expenses, including loan principal and interest, property taxes, homeowners' association dues, contents insurance, and telephone, were $1,401. The homeowners' association dues covered building insurance, interior/exterior electricity, pest control, cable TV, trash collection, water/sewer, exterior building and common area maintenance, and amenities.

Continuing the example, it is assumed that the building will be com-pleted in 18 months, and the condominium will appreciate at approxi-mately 10 percent annually. This type of unit is expected to net $18,000 after payment of the rental commission in the first year, rising to $22,500 in the second year. The forecasted cash flow and value calculations follow:

Annual net rental income	$ 18,000
Less annual expenses ($1,401 × 12)	16,812
Annual cash flow	$ 1,188
Initial reservation fee	$ 5,000
Total down payment (includes $5,000)	38,000
Reservation price	189,950
Forecast value in 18 months	218,400
Forecast appreciation	29,450

This is a sound investment strategy except you cannot inspect the actual unit and amenities when the reservation deposit is made. This shortcoming may be partially offset by viewing the plans such as for the two-bedroom, two-bath condominium shown in Figure 6.2. You may be able to inspect similar units in a prior development built by the same developer. If, on the other hand, the buyer plans to **flip** the unit at closing, the sales and closing costs will erode some of the profit that may have been realized from appreciation over a longer holding period. But your capital is tied up for a shorter time, and your profit is realized sooner. The $29,450 gross profit will be reduced by the amount of the real estate agent's commission and closing costs, which may approach $16,450, leaving $13,000 profit before income taxes.

The keys to this being a successful investment are (1) the strength of demand when you decide to sell the property, (2) accuracy of forecast expenses, (3) rental demand, (4) rental commission, and (5) closing costs. The major "bet" is how much will the property appreciate during the 18-month (or however long it may actually be) holding period. This strategy is attractive in that you do not have to pay any real estate taxes, utilities, etc., during the time between signing the reservation agreement and closing on the purchase.

You should temper your judgment when using a preconstruction reservation to buy a resort property by carefully checking the local market for the pricing on similar or maybe larger existing properties. You may find that some already built homes are less expensive and come with a pool of established rental clients.

Figure 6.2
Condominium floor
plan.

Source: Courtesy of
Wintergreen Resort,
Wintergreen, Virginia.

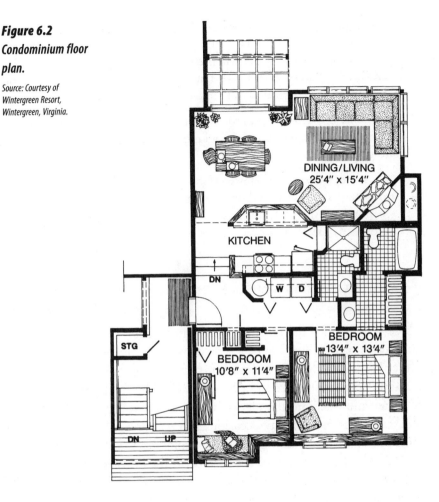

A reservation agreement will probably contain the following six principal sections:

1. *Reservation of unit(s).* This identifies the unit that the Prospective Purchaser desires to buy when it has been constructed and specifies the purchase price.

2. *Deposit of funds in escrow.* This states that the Prospective Purchaser has deposited a specified amount of money as an expression of interest by the Prospective Investor to purchase the unit.

3. *Preloan application.* This requires the Prospective Purchaser to submit a bank application, lender release authorization, and income tax returns generally for the past two years. This information is required in order for the Developer to obtain a construction loan commitment.

4. *Period of reservation agreement.* This notifies the Prospective Purchaser that when the Developer has a sufficient number of executed Reservation Agreements, the Developer will present contracts on a presale basis. The Prospective Purchaser has a set number of days, such as 10, to execute and return the contract with the specified balance of the earnest money.

5. *Termination.* This outlines the conditions under which the Reservation Agreement shall terminate and all monies paid to date shall be returned to the Prospective Purchaser.

6. *Nature of reservation.* This section indicates that the Agreement is not an offer to sell or a binding obligation for the Prospective Purchaser to purchase the unit. Such binding obligation occurs only when the Prospective Purchaser executes a contract for the purchase of the unit.

Previously Owned Homes

These homes offer the advantage of mature landscaping—the planting and nurturing of which can be a time-consuming and exasperating chore. Either in mountains or at the seashore, landscaping may be an expensive trial-and-error experience for a noncondominium home where you need to water and maintain the plants. This may prove impossible since you will only be at the property occasionally. Of course, a local yard maintenance company can maintain the landscaping for a fee.

The price per square foot tends to be lower for older homes than for new homes, plus you may have more negotiating latitude. If, for example, a new home costs $300,000 to build, there cannot be much flexibility in the price charged by the builder or the first owner within the first year or so of ownership. On the other hand, a seller of an older home may have bought it 10 years earlier for $200,000 and now has it listed for $300,000. You can see the older property owner has more flexibility in negotiating a price that you are willing to pay. Remember, there is always the possibility of overpaying for an older home when the costs of remodeling, repairs, new furnishings, and a new HVAC system are added to the purchase price. Older properties may contain space that is not functionally designed, so you will need to decide how useful it is to you and how much value it adds to the house. I once considered a cottage that had a stairway landing the size of a bedroom and cost the same per square foot as the rest of the house to build but was almost useless.

Try to get a house with an open floor plan, especially between the kitchen, dining area, and living room. This design will alleviate the small-room, cut-up appearance and provide a greater feeling of spaciousness. Rental agents tell me that one of the most frequent requests of renters is for a house that is "bright and airy."

It may be advisable to retain an architect to advise you on whether it is possible and relatively inexpensive to demolish a nonbearing wall to open up the dining-food preparation and living areas to modernize a dwelling. You, of course, will want to build into your offering price this renovation cost estimate.

Some of the possible disadvantages of buying an older home are as follows:

✤ The development may have reached the peak of its desirability and its appeal has begun to suffer from houses not being properly maintained

✤ Leaky basements (also possible in poorly designed and constructed new structures)

✤ Termite infestation and dry rot

✤ Foundation settlement (can happen to new construction)

✤ Inadequate electric service

✤ Rusty or clogged plumbing

✤ Outmoded kitchen and bathrooms and insufficient number of bathrooms

✤ Old and inadequate heating and air conditioning system

✤ Under-capacity water heater

✤ Drafty floors, windows, and doors

✤ Roof shingles require replacement

✤ Floor covering requires replacement

ARCHITECTURAL APPEAL AND CONSTRUCTION QUALITY

Often, an older house is cheaper but may not offer as much upside appreciation potential as a newer vacation property. However, if it is well constructed, designed, and maintained and commands an appealing slope-side, ski-in/ski-out, village location, great mountain view or water frontage, its value should continue to rise. Some buyers will accept a building in mediocre condition in order to get an ideal location. Earlier-built units often are on sites with the best views and access to slopes, the beach, or a village center. Don't be afraid of a structure that looks a little rough if it is well designed and constructed and in a strong location. The home can be improved, but virtually nothing can be done to enhance an inferior location. Check the resort master plan and zoning for building height limits or otherwise determine if your million-dollar view will be blocked sometime in the future.

Perceived quality of construction makes a difference in price. A good return on your investment is possible on professionally performed cosmetic remodeling, carpet and entry slate installation, and kitchen modernization. Buy durable, quality furnishings that appeal to a broad segment of prospective renters and owners.

Choosing Among Housing Types

The choices of housing typically include single-family detached, townhouse, and condominium. The first two are easily distinguished from a physical perspective.

Single-family detached residences are located on their own lot, and the owner is responsible for the upkeep of the interior and exterior of the house as well as the yard. The yard may be rather large in areas where land is comparatively cheap or a good part of the property is unusable where there may be wetlands or a mountainside. Some single-family detached residences may be situated on small lots with virtually no side yards on one side in what is known as cluster developments or zero lot line neighborhoods.

This type of home offers privacy from close neighbors with active children or loud stereos blasting throughout the night. These property values tend to appreciate faster than the other two types of housing. An owner has more latitude on building additions to the house than with the other two types. But the owner typically must submit any proposed changes to the building's exterior to an architecture review committee. These committees typically must approve exterior paint color, roofing materials, building alterations, fence design, and removal of trees above a specified diameter.

Before you purchase a home of any type, carefully read the restrictive covenants, which will contain the architectural controls. Remember, you buy a home subject to these controls. In one unusual case, an architect decided to "express his personality" in a house design that clearly was prohibited by the architectural controls. When he insisted that he could build whatever he wanted on *his* lot, he eventually had to tear down the house and reimburse the subdivision board of directors for its court costs. If the development has private streets and a recreation complex, an owner will be liable for annual dues and possibly future special assessments.

The privacy enjoyed by having a yard may generate more work than some owners wish to assume. After awhile, they may lose enthusiasm for mowing the lawn at their principal residence only to continue the process as soon as they reach their vacation home. This prospect may quickly convert owners to believe in mulched areas and no lawns. For some families, these homes are either too large or expensive to maintain. I once was astonished to hear of an owner's guests offering to help with these chores, but it turns out that the cottage owner telling the story was just kidding me.

CONDOMINIUM OR TOWNHOUSE—ARE THEY THE SAME?

Condominiums and townhouses represent legal forms of property owner-ship. At the same time, they may imply different types of residences. Some buyers may be deterred from owning a townhouse or condominium because of the common wall between homes. On the other hand, they may also prefer freedom from the responsibility associated with owning a deta-ched home.

The condominium form of ownership may apply to a detached dwel-ling, townhouse, or often to a single-floor dwelling floor plan in a multi-unit structure. It is much like an apartment building, except the dwellers own rather than rent their homes. For some people, it may be too much like living in an apartment building. Condominiums in resorts often are known as villas. A real estate agent once said, "Never call a condominium a unit; it is a home. Who wants to live in a unit!"

Advantages of owning a condominium are that the price per square foot is less than a detached home and probably less than a townhouse because they are built more intensively, and savings are realized on construction due to economies of scale and more housing units built per acre. The price of a condominium may be 20 to 25 percent less than for a similar size detached home of similar quality construction. Often, condominiums offer superior views and closer proximity to community recreation amenities such as the swimming pool and ski slopes because their more intensive development justifies their being situated on the most valuable land. A big selling point for condos is the ability to walk away from it when your visit has ended and you lock the door. Someone else maintains the lawn and takes care of the exterior maintenance. Although it may take courage for a buyer to be among the first to buy a condo in a new section of a resort, these homes generally perform well in terms of value appreciation.

Disadvantages include lack of privacy and sometimes inadequate soundproofing; it is possible to have neighbors on each side and above and below your home. Yet, in most cases, you won't have all of the adjoining homes occupied during your visit except perhaps during the high season. While condominiums typically are priced lower than town homes and detached homes, their price may not advance as rapidly as these other forms of ownership. The tendency to overbuild condominiums has been greater than that for single-family detached homes.

Before buying a condominium, compare condo association dues at similar developments; check the amount of reserves on hand and assessment or dues trends. Are the existing reserves sufficient to pay for scheduled or needed repairs? Special charges, or regime fees, may be charged to support the regime (neighborhood) infrastructure. Carefully read the condominium regime documents, noting whether any major assessments are scheduled for which you will be liable. An indication of an assessment in the near future may appear in the regime board of directors' meeting minutes. Try to have the purchase agreement state that this assessment is to be paid by the seller or, if by you, have the amount of the owners' assessment reimbursed by the seller and placed in escrow for your future use. Also, determine if there is any prohibition against renting to others.

If you own a condominium, you in effect own a cubicle that extends from the interior of your property's ceiling, walls, and floor. Additionally, you own jointly (in common) with all the other property owners in your development the exterior structure, hallways, elevators, storage areas, and amenities that may include swimming pools, playgrounds, clubhouse, grounds, and walking trails. Since you own these common areas with the other resort owners, you are required to pay a monthly or quarterly regime fee to maintain these features. Sometimes, if the association reserves are inadequate to pay for an unanticipated expenditure, such as repaving parking lots or installing a new roof, you may have to pay a special one-time assessment. This really is no different than what happens with your primary home.

You have seen row houses in older sections of cities. This type of resort home is in a two- or three-story row structure. Each single building will have several dwelling units. A townhouse owner owns the lot on which it rests plus the living unit itself, including the exterior walls and roof, unlike a condominium owner who owns only the inside of his living unit. The townhouse owner will have his individual access versus a common hallway, but like the condominium owner, he probably will have common ownership in the neighborhood amenities, play areas, and parking lots. If there is a homeowners' association, it should be checked out to discover if there are any financial or building structural problems prior to purchasing a property.

Advantages of owning a townhouse over a condominium include the fact that there will be only two adjoining neighbors, and if you own an end unit, just one. Its design fits between a detached home and a condominium in that it typically is priced between the two and offers less privacy than a detached home but more than a condominium. Your ability to change the exterior also falls between the other two forms of ownership. Some people like the added sense of security of the townhouse over a detached property. A townhouse generally will provide a small rear yard and patio, which offer outside living but only requires minimal upkeep.

7 FURNISHED OR UNFURNISHED

MAKING THE CHOICE

Buy the *property*, not the furnishings. But what should you do if one of two similar properties is furnished and the other is unfurnished? Typically, you will be ahead if you buy a furnished property if the furniture and furnishings are in sound condition, of good quality, and satisfy contemporary tastes. The seller inevitably will discount the price that he paid for these items because he probably has no place for them and doesn't want to bother with the hassle of moving them a long distance back home. It is very helpful if you can get a clear idea of the price that similar unfurnished properties command. Using this information, plus an estimate of how much it will cost you to replace particular items, you can make a realistic judgment of how much the furniture and accessories are worth to you above the price of the real estate itself (Figure 7.1 shows a luxurious interior of a western lake home).

Suppose, for example, that the property is offered for $250,000, including furniture and furnishings. Through the real estate agent, you have

Courtesy of Scott Hinerfeld at Slifer Smith & Frampton Real Estate, Vail, Colorado.

Figure 7.1
Vail home interior.

determined that similar unfurnished units are selling for about $225,000. Further, you think that you can use most of the furniture and accessories for another three to four years at which time you probably will have to pay approximately $12,000 to replace nearly everything in the house. Soon after the purchase, you will want to replace some items in order to qualify the property for a rental program. The cost of these immediate replacements is $2,000. Thus, you conclude that you can justify paying around $232,000 ($225,000 + $7,000). The $7,000 is how much value you assign for the use of the furniture and furnishings for the next three to four years, less the $2,000 that you will have to pay out immediately ($9,000 – $2,000).

If the furnishings are not included in the sale of the property, specify in your initial offer that all or some of the furnishings will be included in the purchase price. Generally, some pieces can serve as "starter" furniture, allowing you to use the property now. Then later, you can take time to shop carefully for the desired furnishings at good prices. Talk to property managers and sales persons at local stores who furnish resort properties. Get an idea of the cost to furnish a comparable unit. You will be in a better position to decide how much you are justified in paying for a furnished unit, especially taking into account the age, condition, and appeal of the furnishings.

If you plan to rent the property, seek advice from your tax accountant on whether it is financially advisable on an after-tax basis to depreciate the improvements. If so, get a separate breakdown for the furnishings and appliances, such as $20,000 of the total $400,000 purchase price. You can depreciate these items faster (over five years unless they are replaced earlier) than the structure itself if you choose to do so. Remember, what the government gives, it can take back. That is, any depreciation charged off during the time that you own a property will reduce the tax basis, creating a higher capital gains tax upon the eventual sale of the property. (See Chapter 16 for advice on avoiding capital gains when you sell the property.) Also, you may replace some or all of these items later and be able to write off the replaced items at that time.

The sellers may exclude the furniture and furnishings from the sale of the property or place too high a price on them. If so, state in the purchase contract that they will be responsible for any damage done to the interior of the property when removing the furniture.

If the property does sell with the furniture, invariably, you will not want to keep all of it. If you do remove it, look into either donating it to a charitable organization, such as Goodwill Industries or the Salvation Army, for an income tax write-off or taking them to a consignment shop to be sold on your behalf. Quite likely, neither of these outlets will want some of the furniture and furnishings so you will have to pay someone to haul them away.

Do not leave any old, soiled, out-of-date, and mismatched furniture in the property. You won't enjoy your visits as much, and it will be difficult to rent and especially re-rent it to the same parties in the future. Select colors and fabrics that wear well and do not readily show dirt. Your selections should complement the environment. Furnishings that are appealing for an oceanfront cottage will look out of place in a rustic mountain cabin. Pay particular attention to the style, color, and condition of the carpeting. It may be so dated and stained that it will need to be replaced immediately. But time its replacement with any required interior painting so the new carpeting won't be ruined by the paint crew.

If you plan to place your property in a rental program, invite staff members from two or three rental firms to inspect the unit to give you an idea of what replacements will be required. Sometimes, nearly all of the kitchenware will be replaced by the management firm (at your expense, of course). Frequently, rental agents will recommend that you furnish a vacation

Courtesy of James Boykin.

Figure 7.2
Outer Banks cottage interior.

property with new furnishings of contemporary style, fabrics, and colors (Figure 7.2 shows the interior of an attractively furnished beach cottage). Other likely high-impact replacements are window treatments, bed covers, artwork that depicts an appealing and coordinated theme, lamps, modern entertainment center in the living room plus cable television hookup in two or more bedrooms, and baby equipments such as a port-a-crib and high chair. Ample deck chairs should be provided and, if it is a beach property, several folding beach chairs.

Buy furnishings that will hold up to wear and stains. Buy extra dishes and chair arm covers. King-size beds are popular. Bunk beds allow you to double the sleeping capacity of a bedroom, but as a safeguard, you may want to install a guardrail on the top bunks. Use large scenery prints of beaches or mountains (appropriate for surroundings), and don't use personal pictures.

Have bicycles, maps, restaurant and sightseeing references, maps, emergency instructions, and remedies for sunburn, poison ivy, and sea nettle stings. Alert the guests to not flush nonbiodegradable materials in the toilets (especially for homes on individual septic systems). These items can stop up any toilet and risk overflow damage, which is especially expensive for upstairs baths. Leave TV and VCR operating instructions for renters. Have a good supply of paperback books, videos, and games.

Ingersoll and Davis emphasize having a conspicuous container under the kitchen counter (such as a red bucket) with a stain remover/pet clean-up kit. Further, they recommend that the following statement be included in the renters' book: "Please, **no Kool-Aid or popsicles in the house**: these stains are impossible to remove from furniture and carpets."[26] They suggest using textured ceiling finishes which are less prone to show nail pops and other blemishes. Install a pan with a drain tube for washing machines in case of an overflow; also, use metal guarded washer water hoses.

Bill Fix, broker associate with Great Beach Properties on Seabrook Island, South Carolina, says that, "most women are very astute about design and furnishings while men focus more on size of a property. Over 50 percent of his buyers ask for interior decorating assistance with about half of these using this expertise to affirm their initial design decision."

Generally, the quality and price of furniture and furnishings for vacation properties can be less than you would pay for furnishing your primary residence because it will be used by other guests and possible renters. Further, don't include antiques and family heirlooms that will not survive hard wear. You should not place valuable family furnishings out where they may either be broken or even stolen. As you furnish the property, choose items that are attractive but not likely to break. This especially applies to lamps, decorator bowls, and art objects. An experienced vacation owner from Longboat Key in Florida said, "If you like it, don't put it in your rental property."

Check Resort or Leasing Company's Furnishings Standards

If you are considering placing your property in a resort rental program, be certain to check its required furnishings list against those that may convey with the property to ascertain how much money you will have to spend to replace certain items to bring the property up to minimum standards.

The decorating will differ from your primary home (if you plan to rent it) since you must now focus on maintenance and housekeeping concerns as you cater to hikers, golfers, swimmers, or skiers. In beach resorts, it is advisable to use a wicker-arm sofa over fabric upholstery because of its longer life and stain resistance, especially from suntan oil on hands and arms.

---

[26] Barbara D. Ingersoll and Betsy S. Davis, *Your Home at the Beach* (Bethesda, MD: Cape Publications, Inc., 1998), p. 61.

The rental company/department may encourage you to use nylon, dense-cut, pile carpeting, high-quality sheet vinyl (in kitchens, baths, and foyers), and vinyl wall covering that is cloth or synthetic backed because repairs are virtually undetectable (keep a spare roll of each pattern for future repairs). Use low luster paint on walls rather than semi-gloss, which shows imperfections more readily, and mildew resistant paint in high humidity areas such as bathrooms. Window treatments should be coordinated with the furniture and wall coverings. Shades should be polyester fabric that repels dirt and stains. "Hotel-type" rod pulls are preferred over those with strings, which will break. Generally, ceramic tile should be avoided because of its higher maintenance, especially grout deterioration.

One resort, Wintergreen Resort in the Blue Ridge Mountains of Virginia, recommends for condominiums in its rental program that all furniture be sturdy and functional as well as attractive and coordinated in color and style. Unacceptable furniture items include those made of simulated wood, wood chip, metal composite, vinyl, plastic, crate style, wicker or cane, and homemade or homemade refinished pieces that are not of professional quality. For safety reasons, glass tables with frames or stands are not allowed. Today, attractive lightweight synthetic stone and marble tops are available.

Wintergreen's replacement schedule, based on normal life expectancy, is as follows:

Carpet	Replace every 2–4 years
Furniture	Replace every 5–7 years
Decor/Wall hangings	Replace every 6–9 years
Mattress/Box springs	Replace every 6–8 years

Thus, if you plan to be in a rental program that requires replacements on a set schedule, you are wasting money to buy the most expensive, highest-quality furnishings.

Required Furnishings (per Wintergreen Resort):

A. Living Room:

1. Sofa with coordinated chairs or love seat.

2. Matching end tables and coffee table (bedroom night stands are not permitted in other areas).

3. Enough lamps of appropriate size (26″ minimum height for end tables) to provide sufficient lighting (must be three-way: 50-, 75- and 100-wattage minimum).

4. Properly mounted high-quality pictures.

5. High-quality accessories for tables including silk flower arrangements.

6. Books (paperback or hard cover) are recommended where there are bookshelves.

7. Glass tables are not allowed.

B. Dining Room:

1. Dining table and comfortable matching dining chairs to seat the unit's minimum seating capacity. It must coordinate with living room furniture and cannot be of kitchen, porch, or picnic style. Armchairs are recommended where space allows.

2. Light source sufficient for dining and use as a worktable (hanging light, track lighting, or down lighting).

3. Comfortable, sturdy bar stools that coordinate with other furnishings (if space permits).

4. Properly mounted high-quality pictures.

5. High-quality silk flower or greenery arrangements.

6. Glass tables are not allowed.

C. Each Bedroom:

1. Comfortable beds with frames, box springs, mattresses, and securely attached headboards for two persons. Waterbeds, air mattresses, and platform, bunk, or trundle beds are not acceptable. Good-quality inner spring mattresses are essential.

2. Chest or dresser and matching night stand(s) depending on the bedding and space available.

3. Adequate lighting for reading in bed (three-way lamps, 20″ minimum height above night stand).

4. Properly mounted and appropriately sized pictures.

5. Quality accessories such as silk flower arrangements on dresser or chest.

6. Full length mirror.

D. Patio:

1. Black, brown, hunter green, teak wood, or other approved wrought iron table and chairs to seat minimum of four. (In ocean resorts, non-corrosive furniture is favored over wrought iron.)

2. No cushions or glass furniture allowed.[27]

Additionally, a resort rental department may be expected to require minimum linens, housewares, kitchen equipment, and appliances if they are not provided by the rental service. You may further expect that the rental department will require the property owner to stock specified appliances, kitchen equipment, and housewares, such as stainless steel flatware service.

COST OF FURNISHINGS

The cost to fully furnish a vacation property will depend on the intended formality, size, and quality and whether it is to be included in a rental program. A two-bedroom condominium may cost $12,000 to $15,000 or more for furniture, carpeting, window treatments, linens, and household and kitchenware. Jane Wright, of Manteo Furniture on North Carolina's Outer Banks, notes that a "bare bones" furniture budget of under $10,000 for a four-bedroom cottage is possible—excluding accessories. The price of furnishing tends to rise with oceanfront properties since renters pay higher rentals and in turn expect higher-quality furniture and furnishings. Part of the allure to renting large properties (today, they may be as large as 12 to 16 bedrooms) is staying for a few days in a home superior to that of the renters' own primary home. Part of the appeal is seeing how the rich live. Certainly, lower prices can be found. For example, a furniture company in Fort Myers, Florida, reportedly can provide furniture and bedding for a three-bedroom home for $9,000 to $12,000. Each additional standard bedroom can be furnished for approximately $900 and a master bedroom for $1,400 to $2,000. Another furniture dealer, also in Fort Myers, stated that a three-bedroom condominium can be furnished with moderate priced furniture and bedding for $8,000 to $10,000. For $11,000, accessories

---

[27] "Exhibit D, Property Furnishing Guidelines and Basic Equipment List," *Transient Occupancy Management Agreement for Condominium* (Wintergreen, VA: Wintergreen Resort, January 1, 2004), pp. 18, 20, and 23.

would be included. Furnishings include pictures, lamps, and an entertainment center. Each additional bedroom can be furnished for about $1,200, including table lamps. Low-end furniture typically has lower density foam cushions and fewer springs, which lead to a shorter life and more complaints, especially if the property is in a rental program. Of course, costs will vary by region and quality of furnishings.

Consider using a professional decorator, especially if you value your time. Also, a decorator, having many resources, can "back in" to the amount that you have set in your budget. She can be especially helpful in assisting you to satisfy the furniture/furnishings requirements of a resort rental company as well as knowing from experience which furniture lines best withstand wear and tear from renters and your friends. Most renters expect simplicity, comfort, and attractive furnishings suitable for the environment. That is, furnishings that are fitting for a mountain resort or a waterfront setting. Cheap furniture may either be rejected by the rental company and renters or require your replacing them more frequently than had you bought more durable and higher grade furniture. Avoid lots of frilly, bulky furnishings. These can cause an adverse reaction and clutter the interior of the property. The same caution applies to the temptation of "finally finding a place for the piece of furniture that has languished in your attic for the past 10 years."

Buyers will generally pay something for furnishings, no matter how dated they may be, simply to allow them to immediately use the vacation property. Remember, however, that if you are going to get rid of most of the present items shortly after you have bought the property, then you cannot justify paying much for them—maybe a couple thousand dollars.

8 OWNERSHIP STRATEGIES

BUY LOT NOW, BUILD LATER

It can be argued that it is better to buy and wait than to wait and buy. This is generally true because the population continues to expand while the supply of land is fixed or in some seaside and river areas, it is even decreasing. In other areas, land supply is decreasing because of its being placed in state and national park systems. With the advent of conservation easements, private land is being removed from the market as its future development rights are donated to qualified organizations such as the Sierra Club and the Nature Conservancy. Some of these lands find their way into governmental ownership.

Without being reckless or failing to recognize the various factors influencing the marketability of a recreational lot, it often makes sense to buy a desirable lot as soon as financially possible. Prime lots don't stay on the market very long (see Figure 8.1 for view of a picturesque homesite). A good goal is to pay off the lot and use your equity in it as the down payment when you secure a mortgage on the home to be built later. Otherwise,

Figure 8.1
*Vacant lakefront
lot on Lake Tahoe.*

Courtesy of Cynthia Johnson, SRA, Johnson-Perkins & Associates, Inc., Lake Tahoe, Nevada.

you may be unable to find another lot as appealing and affordable in the future. You may want to consider buying a home prior to retirement and lock in today's prices. It can be leased to help pay off the loan.

If you decide to buy a lot and hold it until you are ready to build or possibly buy and hold as an investment, several things should be taken into account. For instance, on some Atlantic barrier islands that have a history of shoreline erosion from hurricanes and winter storms, it may be advisable to start construction in order to have established the dwelling footprint in relation to the primary dune between it and the ocean. Waiting may result in the lot being unfit for building because the dune line has shifted landward, leaving insufficient building area from a zoning perspective.

A North Carolina real estate assessor recently noted that property values were increasing at a monthly, *not annual*, rate of 1 to 5 percent. Waiting in such markets may put you in a position of playing catch-up—but never doing so. One example of lot appreciation is a $1/2$-acre lot selling for $40,000 in 1973 and for $1.5 million in 2002 (an annual increase of 13.31 percent).

As with virtually any real estate purchase and especially land, specify in the purchase contract that the purchase is contingent upon either public water and sewer (and electricity) being available to the site or an approved septic drain field and reserve field, if required by the local government. The health department or other local approving agency may not grant approval for a desired number of bedrooms. Therefore, also specify the minimum number of bedrooms that you require to be serviced by the drain field. Otherwise, the lot may be approved for fewer bedrooms than you had planned to build. A seven-acre sound front parcel in Kitty Hawk, North Carolina, enjoyed a splendid water view in a picturesque wooded setting, but most of the site was wetlands and would not support a septic disposal system of any kind so no permit could be obtained. Thus, it was not considered buildable and had no value as a home site.

Include in your contingencies, or check on in advance, the availability of federal flood insurance and whether the lot is appropriately zoned. Also, check on the front, rear, and side yard setbacks as well as setback from the primary dunes to assure that you will have a sufficiently large building footprint.

TIMING THE PURCHASE

In most areas, prospective vacation home buyers buy property during the summer. Except for mountain ski resorts, this is the busiest selling and tourist season. If you have the flexibility, it may be wise to wait until the off-season to actively search for a property. Before taking this step, fully use the other seasons to learn as much as you can about the market, studying prices of the type of property you can afford, and even looking at some candidate properties. Some of the properties you were interested in earlier will still be available or will have been withdrawn from the market. Be very careful not to "get cute" about making an offer on an expired listing that was shown to you previously by a real estate agent. The seller probably still is liable to pay the real estate commission, which probably will be reflected in the sales price.

After a property has gone unsold during the peak selling season and the owner faces the off-season maintenance and mortgage payments, they may be more receptive to getting the debt burden behind them before the next season comes around. They have already made a decision to sell but were unable to do so at the advertised price. Now they may be willing to accept a lower offer.

How Should You Own Your Home?

Whole Ownership

Whole ownership occurs when the property owners own the property in its entirety, that is, all 52 weeks of the year. It may be further subcategorized under three forms of ownerships. These are (a) joint tenancy, (b) tenancy in common, and (c) tenancy by the entirety. Key distinctions of these forms follow.

Joint tenancy occurs when real estate is held by two or more persons, with each having an equal ownership. If one of the owners dies, the undivided estate passes to the surviving joint tenants. It may be terminated upon mutual agreement of the involved parties.

Tenancy in common involves the ownership of real estate by two or more persons who have separate and possibly unequal interests. This form of ownership is appealing to unrelated parties since there is no right of survivorship and each person can leave their respective interest to an heir rather than a surviving and unrelated owner.

Tenancy by the entirety is a form of ownership that is limited to husbands and wives and may be terminated by mutual consent of the spouses. Most states view the conveyance of property to a married couple as a tenancy by the entirety. The right of survivorship allows a spouse's interest to be left to the surviving partner. It may provide protection of other jointly held assets where there is no joint debt in case another jointly held investment is foreclosed and the value of the auctioned asset is less than its outstanding debt ("a deficiency sale"). For income tax purposes, each of these three forms allows income and losses to be passed through directly to each owner.

It is always possible to select the resort property that fits your needs and lifestyle, location, etc., and then later, if you would like, bring in other co-owners to reduce your mortgage burden and to create a higher ratio of each party's use versus unused time each year. You should seek counsel from both your tax attorney and accountant on the comparative merits of structuring the ownership of the vacation property. For example, suppose that you are either the sole owner or own a quarter share. Your work schedule restricts your total personal use of the property to two months each year, including weekends. In this example, by being a co-owner instead of a sole owner, your use ratio rises from 2/52 to 2/13. As you can see, your proportion of usage increases as your ownership share decreases, and your ownership costs as well.

Partnership

A **partnership** is an association of two or more persons to conduct a business. Two types of partnerships can be arranged. A **general partnership** is one in which each partner is individually liable for all the partnership debt. This typically is the type used in owning a vacation home with other persons. A variation of this form of partnership is the **limited partnership**. In a limited partnership, the limited partners have no personal liability to creditors, but the general partner does. A major attraction of either form of partnership is that its income and losses are passed through to the individual partners, avoiding double taxation and sheltering other income through allowable partnership losses.

The individual price of an ownership unit decreases as its share of the total property becomes smaller. But its unit value (either by square foot or when all the unit prices are totaled) may rise considerably. For example, an oceanfront condominium may sell for $400,000, but if subdivided into four units of ownership, the total price may reach $650,000 or more. If the same condominium is subdivided into 51 weeks or 51 ownership units, the aggregate price may be $1,000,000. The following illustration is taken from Vail, Colorado, where a quarter share unit sold for $224,500 versus a similar whole share unit for $699,000. Multiplying the quarter-share price by four equals $898,000, but it sold with furnishings, which were worth $40,000, so the premium to the sellers is $159,000 by creating quarter shares. This makes the case for creating a four-party partnership in order to avoid the $159,000 premium. Thus, one strategy, which has been used long before time-shares came onto the scene, is to invite several friends to jointly purchase a condominium, cottage, or cabin. Using this strategy, you can save some of the marketing costs and profits that the developer otherwise would receive.

Before taking this entrepreneurial approach to joint ownership of a resort property, consider the following:

✤ Will the resort or building owner allow this form of ownership?

✤ Will the resort leasing manager assist with the usual maintenance duties and rent the property as aggressively as other properties under her management?

✦ The selection of partners must be done with care to match personalities, decorating tastes, usage, and financial capacity and goals.

✦ It may eventually become burdensome to manage the partnership and keep the relationship pleasurable and profitable. Someone invariably must serve as the "managing partner" and should receive some compensation or a higher percentage of the partnership ownership for this service.

✦ Have an attorney prepare a partnership agreement that enumerates the financial, use, and maintenance responsibilities of the partners, including buyout provisions in case one or more of the partners wants to sell out.

✦ You want to be certain that each partner can financially handle the debt service and will not become overextended and jeopardize the success of your financial interests in the property. It is desirable for all of the partners to have compatible financial strength and goals.

Limited Liability Company

The **limited liability company (LLC)** concept is relatively new. In 1988, the Internal Revenue Service ruled that an LLC can have the same tax flow status of a partnership if certain conditions have been met. It has become popular because it permits single taxation like a partnership and has the limited legal liability of a corporation. The single taxation advantage means that the ownership entity itself is not taxed, but all the taxable income and losses flow through to the individual owners and are reported on their individual tax returns. In forming any legal form of ownership for a property investment, seek competent legal advice. Laws can vary from state to state, so if you plan to own a property in a particular state, you should deal with an attorney in that locality.

Typically, an LLC operating agreement would address the following eight items:

1. *Organization;* stating the company's name and reference to its business address and the company's purpose, such as to purchase, hold for investment, mortgage, operate, lease, refinance, develop, exchange, and sell real property.

2. *Capitalization;* which focuses on the amount of capital contributed by each member and whether they shall be obligated to make additional contributions.

3. *Distributions;* which probably will state that all cash available for distribution shall be on the basis of each member's percentage interest.

4. *Allocations;* this refers to any profit and loss which shall be distributed similarly to that stated in item 3.

5. *Management;* identifies the manager and how he or she is elected and removed; generally specifies the manager's responsibilities, authority, liability, and indemnification.

6. *Accounting books and records;* need to maintain accurate books of account and distribution of financial statements to the members.

7. *Dissolution and termination;* specifies conditions under which the company shall be dissolved.

8. *Miscellaneous;* this section may be devoted to several items, such as "This agreement contains the entire agreement and understanding between the parties . . . and may be amended only in writing by a document duly executed by the members."

Interval Ownership (Time-Share)

The time-share phenomenon has grown remarkably since its advent in the French Alps in the late 1960s. Along the way, there have been snags, especially in the early years when this form of ownership was used to "bail out" motor hotels and condominium projects that had fallen on hard times. Typically, there were scant amenities and comparatively weak sponsorship. Today, there are over 4 million households owning vacation intervals in almost 5,000 resorts in 81 countries. A reason for buying a time-share is to assure your family of future vacations at today's prices at appealing world-class resorts. Unlike in the early years, today's time-shares generally are in high-quality facilities at resorts of your choice. Plus, they provide an opportunity to satisfy your wanderlust by exchanging your week(s) at resorts of your choice. Major brands, such as Hilton, Westin, Hyatt, Embassy, Radisson, Ramada, Marriott, and Disney, have given credibility to the industry. In recent years, the shift has been away from the earlier term "time-share ownership" to "vacation ownership."

The following findings are from a study of time-share pricing in Hilton Head, South Carolina. "Given the choice between renting a unit one week every year for 10 years and buying a one-week time-share in the same property, the time-share provides the buyer with a positive net present value."

The break-even holding period was between five and seven years. "Overall, as a pure investment, time-shares are a very poor use of capital. . . ." "The average rate of return is only slightly higher than 1 percent." "Never 'invest' in a time-share. Use it or lose it."[28]

Urban Land Institute, in its publication, *Developing Timeshare and Vacation-Ownership Properties*, forecast in 1999 that in 10 years, ". . . 20 percent of all U.S. households with incomes of $50,000 or more will be time-share owners, up dramatically from today's (1999) 6 percent penetration rate."[29] According to the American Resort Development Association (ARDA), there are 1,590 time-share resorts in the United States with most of the resorts in Florida (366), California (125), and South Carolina (119). The average price for a time-share week is $14,500, and 3 million U.S. consumers own time-shares.[30] The most common time unit of ownership is one week, with over 90 percent of all time-shares sold in the United States being for this period.

Part of the cost of owning a time-share is an annual maintenance fee. This covers the same sort of expenses that you would expect to pay if you had whole ownership in a resort condominium. These include charges for the maintenance and periodic refurbishing of your unit as well as maintenance of the amenities and also provides for onsite management. The difference is that it would be considerably less than for a full-ownership property. Owners of time-shares often have two areas of concern—with the administration of the homeowners' association and with the potential increase of their annual association fee.

Some units are called **lock-off units**. For example, a two-bedroom unit may be divisible into a one-bedroom unit with kitchen and a second one-bedroom unit with a kitchenette—each having separate entrances. This arrangement offers an owner the flexibility of renting one unit and occupying the other, or depositing for exchange a two-bedroom unit or two separate one-bedroom units.

---

[28] Alan J. Ziobrowski and Brigitte Ziobrowski, "Resort Timeshares as an Investment," *The Appraisal Journal* (October 1997), pp. 379–380.

[29] "Americans Increasingly Desire Recreational Property," *Hotel & Motel Management* (July 19, 1999), p. 22.

[30] "The Timeshare Industry: Facts at a Glance," American Resort Development Association quoting Ragatz *Associates Resort Timesharing in the United States 2003 Edition Summary Report* (August 2003).

Advantages of a Time-Share Vacation Home Interest

1. A whole ownership may cost from $500,000 to $2,000,000, but an owner only uses two to four weeks a year while paying mortgage installments, real estate taxes, insurance, and utility bills for the entire year.

2. You own what you want to use when and where you desire. Thus, it provides more flexibility if you get tired of going to the same place year after year. Your children often lose interest in going to the same place over time.

3. By buying from a sponsor, such as Sheraton, versus a resale unit at a discounted price from an owner via a broker, you may receive marketing incentives such as additional weeks, airline trips, and points in a hotel system. Many of these benefits may be lost with a resale (ask the sponsor's agent and get in writing that you will be able to convey these benefits to a buyer). Some resort sponsors, such as Sheraton, do not sell time-share interests for owners who want to sell.

Sometimes, prices and incentives are better when purchased at preconstruction prices.

Caveats

1. Consider the reputation and financial strength of the sponsor organization. Deal with higher-end and ultimate flexibility brand developments such as those offered through Starwood, Marriott, and Hilton. Larry Hayden, owner of Timeshare Resales *(http://www.vacation-resales. com)*, states that many owners receive only 30 to 50 percent of what they initially paid. "However, resales at premium resorts, operated by such companies as Marriott, Hilton, and Hyatt, can be as much as 85 percent of the original purchase price."[31]

2. Seek a top location and season for optimum exchange. Buy in a strong resort where demand exceeds supply for vacation housing.

3. Plan your exit strategy before you buy a time-share. Determine your options for selling it and whether the resort will assist you. Learn as much about the resale market as you have learned about the initial purchase pricing.

---

[31] John Schmeltzer, "Selling Shares a New Way," *Knight Ridder Newspapers* (July 11, 2004).

Types of Time-Share Ownership The *fixed-unit, fixed-week deeded agreement* is the oldest and most familiar form of ownership. It guarantees an owner use of her unit at a particular resort at the same time every year. It offers nominal income tax benefits and may be used, rented, exchanged, and bequeathed to one's heirs just like whole ownership in a vacation or personal residence. It is important to deposit your week as early as possible in order to give you maximum choice on selecting an exchange week elsewhere. Also, you should request as many resorts in as many time slots as possible. I recall once trying to reserve a week on Florida's West Coast, and only one unit in a resort was available along the entire coast when I wanted it.

The *floating time plan*, instead of allowing the owners to use their condominium at one specific period annually, is more flexible. This plan typically permits the owners to use their property within a broader time zone—perhaps within a season, such as spring or summer. The advantage of this arrangement is that the owners have greater flexibility. You can schedule your vacation for any time within three or four months as opposed to just one week. This form of vacation ownership has increased in popularity to where it now makes up 70 percent of all time-share sales in the United States. However, unlike the assured fixed-unit, fixed-week plan, an owner must realize that reservations are granted in order of when they are made. So if you wait too long making up your mind, you may not get the time period that you want. To increase the odds on your getting the desired week, you may need to reserve it at lease a year in advance, which will not fit everyone's vacation timetable.

The *right-to-use agreement* is quite different from the previous two plans. Here, the developer retains ownership, and the purchaser is able to reserve the right to use his units for a specified number of years when it then reverts back to the developer. This is more like a long-term lease. As you might imagine, the value of these arrangements declines with each passing year since a successor owner will have fewer years to enjoy it.

The *point system* works well if you can gain use of properties in different resorts. This plan may deed an owner rights in perpetuity or for a set term. Points may be purchased and used as currency to reserve time-share accommodations of varying sizes (number of bedrooms) at different resorts for different lengths of stay and even travel services. It is flexible in that you can use part of your week at one time and the balance later. Unused points are automatically banked for the next year, but they may not be saved for more than one year. They may also be borrowed from the next year's allotment, or additional points may be purchased to assemble a sufficient number required for this year's vacation. A given number of points will purchase more days during low-demand seasons than in peak seasons.

Purchasing Time-Share Ownership The American Resort Development Association offers sound advice on buying time-share/vacation ownership in the form of eight tips:

1. *Buy to use* since full usage is the benefit of this form of ownership—not a financial gain as one might expect upon sale of a whole ownership in a cottage or condominium. In fact, you probably will sell it for less than the purchase price.

2. *Choose a vacation that suits your lifestyle.* Give serious thought to what you enjoy most when you vacation. It may be skiing, sunning on the beach, hiking, golfing, tennis, or boating. Look at a variety of vacation products and learn from friends who own time-shares.

3. *Visit a time-share resort on your next vacation.* Tour a resort and listen to the sales presentation, but make it clear that this is the first presentation you have attended and want to compare that plan with others in the area. Try to talk to existing owners and get their candid views on the merits of the resort, plan, resort management, and exchange experience.

4. *Carefully read the documents and ask questions about the product.* Exactly what kind of plan is being offered, and what are your rights and responsibilities?

5. *Ask if the resort is an ARDA member.* Such membership provides you with another level of confidence regarding the quality of services offered.

6. *Look for signs of good management.* Are there friendly and competent services, well-maintained facilities and resort amenities, and good housekeeping?

7. *Ask yourself if you are buying primarily to use the exchange feature.* If so, buy the largest unit in the most popular season or the largest affordable points package available. David Skinner, president of Holiday Groups, says to buy "trading power," or as he states it, "It's more important to buy what everyone else wants, than what you want."[32] Also, learn about

---

[32] David Skinner, "All the Right Places for All the Wrong Reasons," *Timeshare Resales*, http://www.holidaygroup.com/editorial.php.

the resort's exchange policies and with which exchange company it is affiliated. Determine which resorts are the most popular, and purchase your unit there in order to give yourself the maximum choice in exchanging. In descending order, the most popular states for recreation purchase are Florida, California, Colorado, North Carolina, Texas, and Arizona. Preferred settings for purchase are beaches, lakes, and mountains.

8. *Find out how well the resort is managed.* Is it managed by the developer or by a management company? Determine the special assessment history and level and trends of annual assessment. Check the records to determine if there are ample reserves to maintain the resort in its present state. Read several recent homeowners' association newsletters to get a feel for owner satisfaction.

Perhaps the most important guideline for buying a time-share is "Buy when and where everyone else wants to be at a resort." The only thing that will happen to a cheap off-season time-share in a mediocre resort is that your unit will become much cheaper when you attempt to sell it.

When buying a time-share, remember that you have the right to change your mind within a statutory "cooling-off" period. This right is granted to you by state law. In Virginia, for example, you have seven calendar days following the execution of the contract to cancel it. You may rescind (back out of) the purchase without penalty and receive any deposit that you may have made. Know your rights and what this time period is prior to signing a purchase contract. The developer or its agent must be notified according to state regulations. For example, you may have to do so by hand delivering the notice to the principal office of the project or by mailing it by certified U.S. mail, with return receipt requested.

When you are vacationing, check out the prices of new time-shares versus resale units. You may find that the resales can be purchased for half the price of the new units. Larger resorts are represented by brokerage companies that specialize in resales. If you are renting at a time-share resort, check the bulletin board or ask someone in the sales office to see a price list of units available for sale either by owners or the resort.

Time-Share Exchange Companies The two major exchange companies are Interval International (II) and Resort Condominium International (RCI). Most time-share resorts are affiliated with one of these firms. RCI is the largest time-share exchange organization in the world. II is a worldwide operation, has attracted leading resort developers as affiliates, and even provides for exchanges on cruise lines, which usually requires an additional payment by the exchange member. These companies are similar in that both rate the member resorts' time-shares in three time categories, from most popular to least popular. II's ranking is red season (high demand), yellow season (average demand), and green season (low demand). Similarly, RCI's ranking is red season (high demand), white season (average demand), and blue season (low demand).

Exchanging Time-Shares Being able to exchange time at an owner's home resort for a vacation at another resort is an important reason for people buying time-shares. According to the ARDA, more time-share intervals in the United States are used for exchange than for occupancy by their owners. In fact, many owners have never occupied their own time-shares. They bought them as a "trading chit." A 2003 report indicates that 75 percent of time-share owners banked, saved, or traded time to vacation elsewhere.[33] Clearly, the exchange opportunity is the most important motivator for purchasing a time-share. This flexibility is a major attraction for many owners. In fact, a large number of owners have never stayed at their "home resort."

Interval International advises that members (1) decide where and when they want to travel and (2) select an exchange method: either deposit the week first or make a request for an exchange first. You can increase your trading power by depositing your week first and placing an exchange request up to one year before your week arrives. It is recommended when you request an exchange, that you select a minimum of three different resorts and at least one travel date, or one resort and three travel dates. To improve your odds of exchanging even more, select three travel dates and three resorts. You even can select a geographic area to give the travel consultant more flexibility and then decide whether you want to use any of the available resorts.

Alternatively, you can request an exchange first; you then can retain your week until you get a confirmation on your request. Two other arrangements offered by Interval International are the Flexchange and Early Deposit/Early Request programs. The Flexchange program is designed for people who can travel on short notice. You would check on available destinations between 59 days to 24 hours before you intend to travel. An advantage of this plan is the opportunity to upgrade from an accommodation that is equivalent to your home resort time-share. But,

---

[33] Ragatz *Associates Resort Timesharing in the United States 2003 Edition Summary Report.*

there may be limited choices and difficulty in making your travel arrangements. The Early Deposit/Early Request program allows owners to deposit up to two years in advance of their week and to place a request for an exchange time-share two years prior and two years after their deposited week.

Key things to consider when planning to exchange a time-share unit include the following:

✤ Check on the resort rating; for example, II's top rating is a "Five Star" resort.

✤ Find out if the resort has an onsite 18-hole golf course or one within close proximity.

✤ Be willing to exchange for the same size or smaller unit to increase the prospects of obtaining a unit; for example, if you have a two-bedroom unit, state that you will accept any unit that will accommodate the number of people traveling. My wife and I have a two-bedroom lockout unit, but we only need a one-bedroom unit or a studio (particularly if we can visit a dream location).

✤ When trading part of your unit, the size of the private sleeping part determines the size of the unit you may receive. That is, a two-bedroom unit should trade for a two-bedroom unit or perhaps a one-bedroom unit in a popular resort area.

✤ Bank your deposit early in order to maximize your trading power and make your request early—up to one year in advance of your intended vacation.

Getaways An advantage of time-share ownership is the bonus weeks or getaways that are available to owners through exchange companies such as Interval International or Resort Condominium International where you can buy time at participating resorts at reduced rates. II allows you to use up to 12 getaways annually, while RCI sets no limit. They may be used on an unlimited basis. II, for example, allows its members up to 12 weeks annually of getaway time. Arrangements may be made one year in advance of your trip. Although the discount will vary by resort and time of year, the savings may be 25 to 60 percent less than the quoted rental rates. One agent saw some instances where the weekly getaway rate was equal to the resort unit's quoted nightly rental rate. Not surprisingly, availability and amount of discount varies with inventory supply. In higher demand seasons, it is virtually impossible to find accommodations. Yet, in off-peak demand seasons at less popular resorts, you may have success. II, for example, features ongoing specials throughout the year at such resorts as Hilton Head Island, South Carolina, the Maine coast, or Palm Springs, California. Weekly rates can be as low as $274. Size of units will vary, so if your travel schedule is fairly flexible, this could be a good opportunity for you.

Selling Your Time-Share Interest A good source for selling your time-share interest is a firm that specializes in time-share resales in the resort community where your property is located. Several firms may be available so visit all of them to become familiar with their marketing strategy, success, and reputation. These firms can be a good source because some prospective buyers, after having visited new offerings, do not want to pay the full price of a new unit. These people can be prime candidates for your time-share. Determine whether the company holds a real estate license in the state where the resort is located. If you are uncertain about the credibility of the firm, you might check with the local better business bureau or the state real estate commission.

Inquire with the developer or the resort sales office to see if they will sell your time-share. If they are unable to assist you, inquire before you buy what your options are on selling it. Ask to see the resort's bulletin board where present owners have posted units for sale. Is there a resort newsletter where you can post an ad? These two sources are excellent places to advertise since satisfied owners often want to expand their number of weeks of vacationing. If they say you can advertise it yourself or sell it over the Internet, that may be discouraging news since you may have considerable difficulty in obtaining a satisfactory price within a reasonable time frame. In fact, if the developer does not have a resale program, think seriously about whether you should even buy from that resort.

When you decide to sell your unit, get a clear idea of the prices they have been receiving compared to the current advertised prices. Check on the sales commission, and do not be surprised if the price is much less than what you paid and the commission is anywhere from 10 to 25 percent of the sales price. Remember that as much as 30 to 50 percent of the original price may be the cost of advertising and promoting the time-share sales and most, if not all, of this cannot be recouped in the resale market.

You, of course, can advertise in your local newspaper, in a newspaper at the resort where your time-share is located, or in travel-leisure magazines that include a classified real estate section. Check to see if there is a special event in your home resort community during your fixed week. For example, there may be a celebrated boardwalk arts festival or beach music festival that may be of interest to prospective buyers. Numerous resale companies are available on the Internet. Enter the term "time-share resales" on any of the search engines and you will likely discover nearly a hundred firms. One source is *http://www.tug2.net/advice/ts-sales.html*. TUG's classified advertisements cost $10 for three months. Online services such as Prodigy, AOL, and MSN provide fee or low-cost classified ads. A key strategy in successfully selling your unit is to advertise, advertise, advertise!

Be wary of companies that charge a nonrefundable listing fee in advance. This fee may range from $300 to $800. Having received this fee in advance removes much of the incentive to sell your time-share interest. You probably will be disappointed with the results. The better business bureau serving the Buffalo, Niagara Falls, Rochester, Albany, and Syracuse regions offers several important tips such as (1) ask the person calling you or a resale business that you may have contacted on the Internet to send written material, (2) ask where the company is located and in what states it does business, and (3) contact the better business bureau or the state attorney general's office in the state where the company is located to see if complaints have been made against the company.

Private Residential Club (PRC)

A PRC adds attractive amenities, such as a lavish clubhouse and five-star hotel services, that are not available even with wholly owned vacation homes. The club functions like a private golf club where the members are entertained with social events and form social relations with other members.

The PRC is marketed as a real estate investment, not vacation time. The competition is wholly owned vacation real estate and not time-shares. Owners are able to use the facilities at one or more resorts. The high-end fractional ownership really began in 1999. The majority of the units at that time were priced in the $100,000 to $300,000 range.

An example of fractional share units is at Copper Mountain in Colorado; this ski resort opened in the early 1970s. One project there is The Cirque at Copper. These are quarter-share units west of the Village; they sell furnished. An owner is entitled to use the unit one week each month, plus use the facilities 365 days a year, subject to availability. Intrawest bought into this resort in 1997; the first building was constructed in 1999. Usage had grown to 120–140 nights a year by 2002; 65 to 70 percent of the occupancy was rentals.

The most popular units are on upper floors with views; they sell for higher prices than the ground and lower floors. Prices generally rise from $10,000 to $20,000 per floor and the same premium is paid for slope side over the rear side of the building. For example, similar first floor three-bedroom units sold for $640,000 and sixth floor units sold for $800,000. Premium prices were paid for units in the center of activity and those units with ready access to the slopes; lower prices were paid for units adjacent to water features (offering ice skating, board walks, and row boats). The average users are in their early '30s to mid '50s and are a big source of business according to Steve Harriage, broker associate with Playground, an Intrawest Company, at Copper Mountain, Colorado.

Fractional Ownership

This form of ownership involves longer periods of vacation ownership than time-shares, generally ranging from five weeks (1/10 share) to 13 weeks (1/4 share). An appeal of fractional ownership is that it is considerably less expensive than whole ownership, but it offers essentially the same benefits and in some instances much more. Since the average amount of time most whole owners visit a resort is two weeks, a fractional ownership offers a greater usage to cost ratio. The fractional interval is based upon the guaranteed delivery of prime time during the high season, plus additional float time on a first-come, first-served basis during the shoulder season.

Wallace Hobson, CRE, a Portland, Oregon, specialist in resort property, notes that the newest fractional product is an upscale luxury home designed to appeal to the affluent buyer. These luxury products are differentiated from time-shares. Buyers typically are high-echelon professionals and corporate executives who want a high level of luxury and service. They can afford an expensive vacation home, but due to infrequent use they cannot justify the investment. According to Jennifer Martin in "Luxury at Your Leisure" in *Unique Homes: The World of Luxury Real Estate* (no date), fractional ownership programs allow investors to buy shares in upscale homes. They are generally called residence clubs and have mushroomed since the mid-1990s. Busy people like them because they ease the hassles of travel planning. Owners can book time beyond their allotted share, usually for a modest rate. The four major fractional ownership chains are The Ritz-Carlton Club, The Owners Club, Marriott Grand Residence Club, and Four Seasons Residence Clubs. They differ from typical time-share arrangements by featuring full-service staff. Services offered may include the concierge staff arranging for valet pickup at the airport, reserving tee times, and booking the children's ski lessons.

The following sampling of Colorado ski resort fractional ownership products in July 2002 illustrates key features of this form of vacation ownership.

Andrew Woods, broker associate with Hyatt Vacation Club/Main Street Station in Breckenridge, noted that Hyatt offers a 1/20 interest or 17 days per year fractional ownership. This is a five-star resort with high-level amenities. Owners can stay at other Hyatt resorts such as in Hawaii, Mexico, the Caribbean, British Isles, Denmark, Switzerland, or Australia. It also allows owners to use their memberships at Hyatt hotels.

In Breckenridge, Hyatt sells only winter weeks, i.e., seven days plus 10 days either in the spring, summer, or fall. You should buy a fractional or time-share in a strong demand resort and in a strong demand time zone in order to assure strong exchange demand and value. Since Hyatt has relatively few resorts and fractional shares, demand is strong in the resale market.

With a Hyatt 1/20 fractional ownership share, an owner receives a fee simple deed for 17 days usage per year (one winter week plus 10 days during remainder of the year). In 2002, prices ranged from $30,000 for a 400–500-square foot studio, to $60,000 for a 1,000-square foot two-bedroom unit, to $90,000 for a 1,400-square foot three-bedroom unit. The annual homeowner's fee for a two-bedroom unit in 2001 was $1,758 per year. This included real estate taxes, insurance, Interval International membership, maid service, furnishings, utilities, and refurnishing every 3–5 years. This fee is broken down into 80 percent for operating expenses and 20 percent reserves.

A two-bedroom unit may rent for $525 a night in the winter, with 65 percent going to the owner and 35 percent to a third-party management firm.

The Interval International exchange fee was $149, plus a $29 Hyatt exchange fee, and a $49 guest fee.

According to Betsy Edwards, membership executive in Beaver Creek, Colorado, the Ritz-Carlton Club in Bachelor Gulch Village offered two-bedroom residences with 12 memberships per residence. An initial purchase price plus an annual fee covered all utilities, operations, insurance, reserves, property taxes, snow removal, and refuse collection. Membership services include a concierge service to arrange member ski and golf instructions, guided hikes and fishing trips, dining reservations and golf tee time reservations, pre-stocking groceries to members' personal preferences, and twice-daily housekeeping service. Prices ranged from $200,000 to $265,000 for a two-bedroom unit, with mountain-view units bringing 7 to 18 percent more than valley views. Three-bedroom residences range up to $350,000, with mountain views commanding 8 to 25 percent more than valley views. This vacation ownership is marketed as a way of combining pride of ownership of a luxury second home without the accompanying maintenance burdens of whole ownership. To date, Ritz-Carlton only has a few other club locations in St. Thomas Island, Virgin Islands, Aspen Highland, Colorado, and Jupiter, Florida.

9 SELECTING A REAL ESTATE AGENT

Before making a choice, interview several agents[34] to determine if the relationship "feels right." How long have they been in sales in this market? Are they knowledgeable about the area and the type of property that you want to purchase? Do the brokerage firm and agent specialize in vacation property sales rather than primary home sales? Is the office at the resort or in a nearby community? Determine what services will be offered before purchase and up through the **closing**. This is when the title to real estate is transferred from a seller to a buyer; all of the necessary documents are accumulated and funds disbursed, and the deed of trust or mortgage is recorded in the public records. It often has been said that the most difficult part of a real estate agent's work is going from the stage of a written offer

---

[34] It may be helpful to define real estate agent, real estate broker, and REALTOR®. Both an agent and a broker are licensed and regulated by a state board or commission. An agent may either be an employee or independent contractor, but in effect works under a broker who generally owns the realty firm. A REALTOR® is a sales agent or broker, but additionally is subject to the Code of Ethics of the National Association of REALTORS®.

to the closing. This is why you want to select a capable and resourceful agent so that the transaction up to and at closing is worry-free.

The company's name is no guarantee of good service; it ultimately depends on the individual agent. You might even talk to some local people who are familiar with different agents. Unless requesting a specific agent, you usually will be assigned whoever is on floor duty when you walk into a realty firm's office. As you consider several prospective agents to work with you, look for one with whom you are comfortable, has good negotiation skills, keeps you up to date on new listings that meet your criteria, and promptly returns your telephone calls and e-mails.

Is the company a member of the local multiple listing service (MLS), particularly if it is a resort-affiliated firm? You should be exposed to viewing all listings offered by the resort firm and non-resort-affiliated firms as well. Ask the agent if he is prepared to show you all resort home listings, not just his own or his firm's properties.

With buyers becoming better informed about available listings, especially via the Internet, it is less likely that a seller's agent will not show all available listings whether they are his or other agents'. The buyer may already be aware of other agents' listings, and the failure to show them only discredits the agent for failing to make them available to a buyer.

Another source on agents who specialize in vacation home sales is the National Association of REALTORS®, which has a specialist classification, RS. These resort specialists facilitate the buying, selling, or management of properties for investment, development, retirement or second homes in resort, recreation, or vacation destinations.

Should You Be a Customer or a Client?

A **customer** is a person who wants to buy real estate but who has not established an agency relationship and is not represented by an agent. Before proceeding, note that an agency occurs when either a buyer or seller delegates the right to act for and represent their best interests in a real estate transaction. Even without an agency having been established, an agent is required by law to treat a customer fairly and to disclose known material facts about the property and to promptly present all offers from prospective buyers to the seller. However, the agent is not required to negotiate the most favorable price for the buyer. The agent/licensee owes her utmost loyalty to the seller who is her client.

A **client** is a person who has established in writing an agency relationship with the agent and has agreed to be represented by a brokerage company. This written agreement should clearly outline the obligations of both parties. Be certain that the agency relationship is clearly explained to you.

DUAL AGENT

This agency arrangement allows an agent or firm to represent both the seller and you, the buyer. Typically, the seller has already listed the property with a firm. The agent is expected to represent both sides of the transaction fairly. Sometimes, it is difficult for an agent to be completely neutral in these transactions. A seller can forcefully restrict his agent from divulging certain sensitive information to the prospective buyer, such as the lowest price he will accept. This form of agency would most likely occur when you become interested in a house already listed by your buyer's agent or with the agent's firm. The agent would be expected to ask you to sign a separate agreement that permits him to act as an agent for both you and the seller. He is no longer your exclusive agent, must not disclose to either party confidential information obtained from the other party, and cannot serve as an advocate for either party or negotiate for or advise either the seller or buyer as to price or terms.[35] Since this agent is representing two parties with competing interests, it is essential that you clearly understand: (1) what your relationship is with the dual agent and (2) what the agent will do for you in the transaction.

A release from this "divided loyalty" may be for a firm to use a "designated agency" where one agent in the firm represents the seller and another agent acts on behalf of the buyer. Alternatively, you, the buyer, may ask to be a customer and not sign an agency agreement.

BUYER'S AGENT

A **buyer's agent** can help you prepare and submit on your behalf an offer to the seller. His primary duty is to assist the buyer in making an informed decision. Read the agency agreement and fully understand its terms before

---

[35] *Agency Relationships in Real Estate When Buying or Selling Real Estate, Are You a Customer or Client?* From a brochure published by the South Carolina Real Estate Commission.

signing it. One point that you must be clear on is the compensation arrangement. Determine who pays the agent's sales commission. It may be that the agent initially expects to receive his commission from the seller or the listing agent but will seek compensation from you if the listing agent refuses to pay.

An exclusive buyer's agent can help you see a large number of prospective properties, advise you on a realistic price, assist you in selecting the best loan for your situation, help find a reputable home inspector, assist you in negotiating the lowest price, help find the most suitable loan terms, and in general, guide you through the home purchase process. His fiduciary obligation to you should ensure that your purchase offer includes the necessary provisions to protect your interests.

An agent's knowledge of the local market can prove helpful in advising you on a realistic offer for a property. One way that an agent can be especially helpful is to provide you with a **comparative market analysis (CMA)**. This not a full-blown appraisal report, but nevertheless it will identify several recent sales of similar homes. It likely will include the following information about each sale: sales price and original listing price, date built, number of bedrooms and baths, square footage, type of views, extras such as covered decks, swimming pool, hot tub, whether it sold furnished or unfurnished, approximate time on the market, condition of property, and date of sale. A CMA may also list some similar properties that are now on the market. Finally, it will probably state a suggested price range for the property on which you plan to make an offer.

Every resort has "super stars" that may not necessarily be your best bet as a buyer's agent in finding a vacation home. They have their own inventory of homes to move. After you have had agency explained to you, there is no obligation to sign a buyer agency or any other form of agency agreement immediately. You may want to wait until you have viewed several properties with the agent and decide if you wish to be represented by her.

The North Carolina Real Estate Commission's pamphlet "Working With Real Estate Agents" states that a buyer's agent in representing a buyer must:

1. promote your best interests,

2. be loyal to you,

3. follow your lawful instructions,

4. provide you with all material facts that could influence your decisions,

5. use reasonable skill, care, and diligence, and

6. account for all the monies that she handles for you.

You should avoid telling the agent anything that you do not want the seller to know until you have a written agreement with the seller. If you decide to make an offer on a property, the agent must obtain a written agency agreement. If you choose not to sign the agreement, he can no longer represent you and is not obliged to keep any privileged information between the two of you confidential any longer. Perhaps of even greater significance, this agent may seek compensation from you if you later buy through another agent a property that he first showed to you.

Some agents will be members of the Real Estate Buyer's Agent Council (REBAC). This organization is an affiliate of the National Association of REALTORS®, and its Accredited Buyer Representative (ABR) designation is geared toward agents who want to enhance their buyer representation skill and provide proof to prospective buyer-clients of their proficiency at servicing the special needs of buyers. An ABR may be located in the area where you are searching for a vacation property by contacting (800) 648–6224 or visiting *http://www.rebac.net*.

Remember, you have certain responsibilities to an agent. You must be honest in what type and price house you want. This will allow the agent to more readily narrow the search to the very best candidate properties and save all of you time. Be loyal. Don't mislead your agent and don't use several agents. This deception will haunt you as they find out that you have "gone behind their back" to use other agents. Also, once you know what type and location property you want, share this with the agent. Be specific and you will more quickly find the vacation property that you want.

10 Negotiating the Purchase and Sale

When you submit a contract to an owner, do not load your offer with a dozen contingencies so that the owner will not consider it a serious offer to purchase the home. More than one offer has been rejected, even though the buyer met the sales price requirements, because it was laden with pesky clauses that made the owner uncertain of whether the buyer was really serious. Nevertheless, an offer should include the following three contingencies: (1) you must be able to obtain suitable financing, (2) the property must be appraised for at least the purchase price, and (3) the property must pass all inspections or be repaired at the seller's expense.

Once you have visited several properties and found one that fulfills your criteria, make a formal written offer to purchase it. Some people think they can make a verbal offer through the seller's real estate agent in order to accelerate the process or to see if the seller will accept their offer. Most agents with good reason will advise their clients not to even respond to a verbal offer. The seller has almost nothing to gain from doing this and does not know if the prospect even qualifies for a mortgage to buy the property. Plus, it may let other prospective purchasers learn that the offering price is not the stated $350,000, but rather $335,000 that was accepted by the seller. Also, the prospective buyer may be under no obligation to follow through on the purchase since none of this was in writing.

Write down and share your criteria with the agent. In fact, allow him to modify it. You, for instance, might discover that the amenities, location, and size requirements cannot be met. Set up a file of the properties that you like and get from the agent or take your own pictures and notes, including your ranking. Do not disable yourself through "analysis paralysis." The negotiating process eventually has to come to an end. One prospective buyer, who had narrowed his interests down to two properties after having inspected several homes the previous weekend, called the agent only to learn that both had already been sold.

What Is an Acceptable Offer?

Three major conditions will guide you in making this determination. First, after having gained some knowledge of prices that similar properties have recently brought as well as current listing prices, you will know whether the property is fairly priced. Second, has the property been listed for a long time? Third, is the seller highly motivated to sell in order to move elsewhere, avoid foreclosure, or solve some other financial problem by selling quickly?

Rarely will you want to offer the full asking price. But, in some strong sellers' markets, you may have to do so, especially if you have already lost a couple of properties to other buyers who were willing to make full-price offers. Going to the other extreme, you will probably not even get a **counteroffer** from an owner if you offer a ridiculously low price. So where does this leave you? If you offer somewhere between 5 and 10 percent under the listing price, you usually will get a counteroffer. Then perhaps you and the seller will compromise on a price midway between the offering price and your offer. Let's say the property is priced at $400,000 and you make an initial offer of $360,000. The seller may counter at $390,000, with an eventual final price of $380,000 being agreed to by both parties. Motivation to sell or buy a vacation property is so important in the price that is eventually agreed upon. The seller may have grown tired of maintaining the property, the children no longer visit it, vacation interests may have changed, the owner may be moving to a more distant section of the country, or maybe his investment goal has been achieved. On the other hand, the buyer is tired of looking and wants to have a cottage for the upcoming season, the property is in immaculate move-in condition and the seller will let the furnishings go with the house, the price fits within their budget, and it has a wonderful view.

RIGHT OF FIRST REFUSAL

You may spot a vacation property but are not quite ready to acquire it. Perhaps you have other financial obligations that must first be satisfied. For example, you have another three years remaining on a second mortgage on your principal residence, an automobile loan almost paid off, and two more years of tuition to pay on your younger child's college education. Yet, you have found your dream house on the lake, but neither you nor the owner is quite ready to convey the property. One way to reserve the opportunity to buy the property in the future is to use a **right of first refusal**. A right of first refusal is an agreement between a property owner and a prospective purchaser. It can be confusing so you should retain an attorney to advise you. Some agreements may allow a prospective buyer to buy the property before it is offered on the open market through a broker. Other agreements may simply allow the buyer to match another legitimate offer. Generally, it requires that the owner give the buyer the first opportunity to buy a property on the same terms and conditions in legitimate offers that are acceptable to the seller. You, the prospective buyer, then have the right to match the offer or refuse it. If you refuse the price and terms, then the owner has the right to sell it to the party having made a legitimate offer.

Julie Garton-Good offers the following sound advice:

The right of first refusal clause protects you and the seller by stating that: "the seller's property will be kept on the market and should another acceptable offer be received, the seller will notify the buyer in writing, and the buyer will then have 'X' amount of days from receipt of notification to remove the contingency and perform on the contract. Failure to do so will declare this purchase agreement null and void with return of buyer's earnest money."[36]

---

[36] Julie Garton-Good, "Buyers: Use the 'Right of First Refusal' Clause as Ammunition in the Purchase Agreement," *Realty Times—Real Estate News and Advice*, http://www.realtytimes. com, September 29, 2000.

Be certain that a reasonable time is specified for you to remove the contingency. Probably seven to 10 days will be acceptable. Also, require the owner to communicate via a carrier like UPS or Fed Ex that uses a return-receipt system of notification so you will be assured of when your period to remove the contingency has begun.

A right of first refusal is similar to an option, but different. A holder of the right of first refusal cannot force a property owner to sell to him, but only has the right to buy the property at the same price and terms that the owner is willing to accept from other prospective buyers. An **option**, however, gives the option holder the right but not obligation to buy a property at a specified price and within a stated time period. The prospective buyer may exercise the option, renew it, or allow it to expire. The option monies may be forfeited, depending on the language in the option. You should always try to have this money applied to the purchase price if you exercise the option.

Some owners will not accept a right of first refusal because it may impair the marketability of the property. Brokers may refuse to list the property with this condition because they may receive no commission if the holder of the right exercises this right. A more acceptable approach to an owner is for the prospective buyer to gain the **right of first negotiation**. This will not affect the marketing of the property to third parties since the negotiation period ends before the property is listed with a broker. This arrangement simply requires that the owner notify the holder of this right that she intends to sell the property and the two parties have a specified period of time to negotiate a mutually acceptable transfer.

GATHER FACTS ABOUT THE PROPERTY

When buying, check to see how long a property has been on the market and how much time is left on the listing. The buyer may be more motivated to entertain a lower offer toward the end of the listing period when the listing agent will work harder to persuade the seller to consider your offer.

Whether or not you are negotiating directly with the seller, you should know as much as possible about the property. You will already have inspected the property and perhaps had a professional home inspector do the same but in more detail.

You should have reviewed the restrictive covenants and/or condominium regime bylaws, learned whether short-term rentals are allowed, determined the amount of the real estate assessment and annual taxes, reviewed the rental history, reviewed the operating statements for the past three years or so, and learned the value of similar properties. From this knowledge comes confidence.

As you move toward making an offer on a vacation property, consider several items that might enter into the negotiations. Of course, the key issue may be expected to be the price, followed by the date of possession, extent of repairs paid for by the seller, and transfer of furniture and furnishings.

NEGOTIATING STRATEGIES

Of paramount importance is knowing where you want to be at the end of the negotiations. Just remember how much you can justify conceding before the transaction no longer is feasible for you. A good way to proceed is to establish a range of acceptable outcomes, beginning with the most desirable.

Be able to handle frustration, stay on course for your desired outcome, and never become emotional, display anger, or in any way belittle the seller or the property. Similarly, keep your personality and ego out of the negotiations. Negotiations are about buying the property and not about the seller or you. Therefore, stay focused on consummating the transaction.

Whether you are dealing through a broker or directly with a seller, try to avoid establishing a set sequence where a particular issue must be resolved before moving on to the next issue. This can become frustrating for the seller. Deal with and resolve issues as they arise—remembering all of the issues that you want to satisfy before you have a deal. This approach will give you more flexibility in the negotiation process.

As early as possible, help the seller relax and begin to trust you. If you are dealing with a married couple, continually make eye contact with both the husband and wife. As you proceed with the negotiations, resist the temptation of being a "sharp trader." Most people react negatively to a "deal squeezer," where every single aspect has to be on his terms. A highly respected attorney who has been responsible for rezoning numerous parcels says, "A contract is just as enforceable when signed in ink as one signed in blood." Stated differently, always try to allow both yourself and the seller to achieve a satisfactory agreement. Otherwise, there may be no agreement at all. Real estate professionals are fond of describing a well-negotiated deal as a "win-win" negotiation where both parties have achieved acceptable goals. It has been said that, "A successful negotiation is a relaxed search for common ground. If one party is treated unfairly, it is not a negotiation; it is a holdup."[37]

Many times, you have heard that a good communicator is a good listener. Being a good listener is an especially valuable asset in negotiating. Listen and learn what the seller's "nice-to-have versus must-have" goals are. Do not talk too much. That can annoy many people to the point where they will begin to tune you out. An incessant talker may become so overbearing that the seller will stop negotiating just to get rid of him. Being silent at strategic times can put pressure on the seller to respond. Silence can be an effective negotiation device. On the other hand, you may have to bring a talkative seller back to the agenda, getting closure on each point of negotiation before moving on to the next item. Periodically, you might want to review the progress that you have made.

Generally, low-ball, frivolous offers are a waste of time. You walk a fine line in that you can make your lowest offer only once, but you don't want to make it so low that the owner will dismiss it as not being a serious offer. A reasonable offer may be expected to prompt a counteroffer from the seller. Be able to defend your offering price by referring to other similar properties that have sold recently or to some that are still available for purchase.

Set a time limit on your offer to purchase a property. Little can be gained by allowing a seller more than 48 hours to respond to your offer. Some may claim they need the weekend to consider your offer or they will be out of town for a few days. Neither of these are valid reasons to delay their response to a legitimate offer. The danger in allowing a delay is the possibility that the seller either will use your offer to get a higher offer from another party or even to use another offer to increase your last offer. This other offer may not be completely acceptable to the seller because of some problem such as a requested delay in the closing date or a weak financial position. If your offer is rejected, ask the seller or his agent why he thinks it is unreasonable.

MAKING THE COUNTEROFFER

A counteroffer is a modification of the original offer. It is a technique to keep the negotiations alive. It can be made by the seller once you have made your original offer. Also, you can counter their counteroffer. This process is

---

[37] Robert Perkins, "Effective Real Estate Negotiating," *Real Estate Today* (May 1981), p. 48.

based on some part of a prior offer having been accepted. If some part of a counteroffer has been accepted, progress is being made. Often, after several counteroffers on the price, the two parties will agree to split the difference. Don't be obsessed on getting the price you initially wanted if it would cause the seller to cease negotiations out of exasperation because he feels he has been bullied into making too many concessions or feels the transaction is one sided. Never disclose to the real estate agent the maximum price that you are willing to make.

Try to avoid making immediate counteroffers. You may say something that you later regret, seeming to be argumentative, or make an unnecessary concession. At times during the negotiations, you will do well to make your point and stop talking. You may initially be repulsed by an offer. Instead of arguing over the point, compose yourself and ask a question to clarify the point and allow the seller to modify his stance on that point. You might say that you would like to find a different position that you both would be comfortable with.

You should expect to make a concession if you ask for one. But don't make large concessions since the seller will expect more of the same. By making small concessions, you will begin lowering the seller's expectation of what you are prepared to concede on subsequent points of negotiation. If you do make a generous concession, be firmer on the next point.

Final Agreement

Once terms that are acceptable to both parties are reached, the agent can draw up a purchase contract for signatures. Up to this point, you and the agent probably have been working from a legal pad, making revisions as the negotiations progressed and likely all this has been accomplished in no more than three meetings. Alternatively, you can simply work down through the purchase contract, making changes and initialing them and then have the real estate broker submit the changes to the seller for approval and initials. As you remove contingencies, the broker should inform the seller that you have done so. This will keep him informed and indicate progress. You want to move deliberately but not so fast as to make mistakes or appear too eager to acquire the property or so slow as to antagonize the seller or allow an intervening offer to be placed before the seller.

11

RAISING CAPITAL
FOR THE PURCHASE

The overall question when financing the purchase of a vacation property is, "How much can you afford to pay?" The answer has two components. The first affects both the size of the mortgage payment and the magnitude of the loan. (This is the subject of this chapter—raising money for the down payment for the purchase.) Next, you need to know how much can you borrow. This depends on the size of the mortgage payments that your income or the combination of your personal income and the rental income that the vacation property will likely produce.

The different sources of a down payment may be used independently or together with one or more of the other sources of capital. Sometimes, you might be able to pledge other real estate or securities as the down payment. A second mortgage on another property or a **home equity loan** may also be possibilities to explore. Another source of capital is a line of credit based on the strength of your personal financial statement.

A deferred tax exchange is not strictly a means of a down payment. But, it is an excellent way to preserve capital by delaying payment of **capital**

gains tax on the sale of a property, except for a personal residence. There is a required holding period of an investment property prior to exchanging it and specific guidelines for making a property exchange. It is possible to conserve nearly all the money received in the sale of a vacation residence by using this technique.

PLEDGING OTHER PROPERTY

For a variety of reasons, a vacation home purchaser may lack the required down payment. For instance, she may have her money committed to other well-performing investments, there may be severe withdrawal penalties to cash in certificates of deposit or bonds, or her assets may be illiquid and converting them to cash quickly would necessitate a substantial discount for a quick sale. However, most of these assets could be readily pledged as collateral for the down payment providing the mortgage lender is willing to accept them. *The 2002 National Association of REALTORS® Profile of Second-Homeowners* survey found that most buyers use their savings for the down payment of a second home (41 percent), followed by sale of stocks and bonds (8 percent), equity from other homes (5 percent), or a loan from a financial institution (5 percent). Less often used sources are inheritances (4 percent), gifts from relatives or friends (4 percent), sale of investment property (2 percent), and a loan from pension/401(k) plans (1 percent).[38]

You may be able to handle the mortgage payments on the purchase of the vacation property, but for any of the reasons mentioned previously, at the moment you cannot assemble the required down payment. This lack of funds can be resolved if, for example, the prospective buyer owns a debt-free property such as a primary home, office building, or timber tract, for example, that is worth $400,000 and the agreed-upon price for the vacation property is $300,000. By placing a 75 percent loan on any of these three properties, there would be sufficient money for an all-cash purchase of the vacation home.

---

[38] *The 2002 National Association of REALTORS® Profile of Second-Homeowners* (Chicago, National Association of REALTORS®, 2003). Used with permission.

Second Mortgage on Principal Residence

It is possible to withdraw equity from your primary residence by placing a second mortgage on it. This is sometimes known as a home equity loan since you are borrowing on the equity accumulated in your home. A second mortgage is a junior lien on real property. In case of foreclosure, it will be paid off after the first lien is satisfied, and only then if there is any money left over after the foreclosure action is completed. Since it is in a riskier position than a first lien, it commands a higher interest rate. Second mortgages are most commonly used when a purchaser lacks sufficient funds for a down payment. Suppose the required down payment is $100,000, but the prospective buyer only has $75,000. The seller may take back a $25,000 second mortgage to provide the required funds for buying the property. Since the interest rate is higher and the repayment term much shorter than for a first mortgage, the monthly payment will be relatively high in relation to the amount borrowed. Find out if the first lien holder will allow the additional payments on the second mortgage. It may not allow it because the additional mortgage payments could jeopardize repayment of the first lien.

Unless the first mortgage on the primary residence has been completely paid off, it may not be financially prudent to encumber your primary home with additional debt. First, it adds more financial risk since neither the first or second lien on the primary residence will have been paid off. Plus, it may jeopardize repayment of the new loan on the vacation property. Repayment of three mortgages may be unacceptable from a loan underwriting perspective. However, if the loan on the primary home has been fully amortized, there is a reasonably good chance of the vacation property appreciating, and the first mortgage lender and you are comfortable with your ability to make both payments, then it may make sense to place a second mortgage on your primary home. This money can be used for the down payment on the vacation home. Later, you might refinance the vacation home with a first lien sufficient to repay the second lien on your primary home. If you sell your primary residence and then move to the vacation property as your primary residence, you could pay off the second loan balance with the net sale proceeds.

LINE OF CREDIT

If you have a sizeable personal net worth, you may want to consider using it as collateral for the down payment to purchase a vacation home. A **line of credit** is provided by a bank to a customer in the form of a loan of a specified amount over a given period. It is easier to obtain if you have a solid credit history and have a business relationship with the bank. It works like this: you meet with a bank officer and outline your financial needs and present a current personal financial statement. Imagine that you need $100,000 for the down payment on the purchase of a beach cottage. Although the value of your assets exceeds that amount, you prefer not to liquidate them. So you would request the $100,000 for your house down payment. The bank will search your financial statement for appropriate assets that can collateralize the line of credit. Retirement accounts, for example, would be excluded. A bank typically will advance 75 percent of the value of the pledged security. During the time that it serves as collateral, you cannot sell that particular asset.

A line of credit offers the advantages of a lower cost of funds, fewer legal expenses than a second mortgage, the bank may not require title insurance, flexibility, and ease and speed of arrangement.[39] A variation of this financial arrangement is the home equity line of credit where you may borrow against the equity in your home. Typically, the terms are flexible and may involve interest-only payments.

TAX-DEFERRED EXCHANGE

IRC Section 1031 Tax-Deferred Exchange provides another way to buy a second home using almost any property *except one's principal residence*. By buying a vacation home in this manner, you can conserve capital by deferring payment of taxes on the transfer of a property that you sell. This allows you to acquire a more valuable property since you have more money available for the down payment.

---

[39] More detail on a line of credit may be found in James H. Boykin and Richard L. Haney, Jr., *Financing Real Estate* (Englewood Cliffs, NJ: Regents/Prentice Hall, Inc., 1993), pp. 375–377.

Typically, four parties are involved in a tax-deferred exchange: (1) the exchanger (person who is disposing of a property), (2) the buyer of the **relinquished property** (property that belonged to the exchanger), (3) the seller of the **replacement property** (the property that the exchanger wants to acquire), and (4) an intermediary (party who implements the exchange).

An exchange may take place when the exchanger has not identified another property to be acquired at the time the relinquished property is transferred to the buyer. (The relinquished property is the property that the taxpayer initially owns and wants to dispose of in the exchange. Replacement property is the property that the taxpayer receives in the exchange.) Many million-dollar resort homes today were acquired by persons who exchanged a business property, land, timberland, etc., for their resort homes—often as they approached retirement. A **tax-deferred exchange** simply is where a property owner can trade one property for another without having to pay federal and state income taxes on the transaction. It is an exchange of property where, by agreement, a seller transfers *property held for productive use in a trade or business or for investment*. This criterion is a critical test both for the relinquished property as well as the acquired property. Thus, the acquired vacation property should meet the test of being an investment property to qualify initially as an acquired property and later as a relinquished property. The seller of the first property, a.k.a. exchanger, relinquishes title for one property and then receives a replacement property(ies) to be held for productive use in a trade or business or investment.

Required Holding Period Prior to an Exchange

Although the Tax Code requires that property must be held for productive use in a trade or business or investment, the length of the holding period is uncertain. Asset Preservation, Inc. notes that, "In one private letter ruling (PLR 8429039), the IRS stated that a minimum holding period of two years would be sufficient." It further comments that, ". . . there are many advisors who believe two years is a conservative holding period, provided no other significant factors contradict the investment intent."[40] These

---

[40] Asset Preservation, Inc., *How to Benefit from the "Power Of Exchange"* (Granite Bat, CA: Asset Preservation, Inc.), p. 21.

deferred exchanges are reported on IRS Form 8824 "Like-Kind Exchanges." By exchanging one property for another, the exchanger is able to defer capital gains taxes at the time of sale. Assume the following facts:

Sales price		$500,000
Original cost	$350,000	
Depreciation claimed to date of sale	50,000	
Adjusted tax basis		300,000
Capital gain		$200,000
Federal income taxes:		
$50,000 @25%*		$12,500
$150,000 @15%		22,500
Total federal income taxes		$35,000

*If the taxpayer were in a lower bracket, lower rates would apply.

Assuming you can borrow 75 percent on another property bought with the sale proceeds, payment of the capital gains tax now reduces the value of a replacement house that you could afford to purchase by $140,000 ($35,000/25% down payment). Delaying the payment of these taxes for awhile may also allow you to avoid waiting until you have saved more money or liquidated other assets (possibly at a loss) in order to afford a vacation home.

Guidelines on Deferred Tax Exchanges

The basis in the replacement property (the property received) is the same as the basis in the relinquished property (property that was transferred). This is an important consideration if you have a low basis (undepreciated value of improvements) in the relinquished property. This is of greater concern if you have depreciated that property over a number of years. However, it should not be of concern if you are exchanging a business property or possibly another resort property, which has not been depreciated at all or not by very much. A simple rule of thumb is: *In order to totally defer capital gains in an exchange, acquire a replacement property that is of equal or greater value than the relinquished property.* Further, all of the net equity must be reinvested in a replacement property having the same or greater debt.

The basis in the new property that you have exchanged into will be increased if you pay money ("boot") in order to balance the sums of the two exchanged properties. This will, of course, increase your basis for depreciation. In other words, you will be able to charge off more depreciation annually for tax purposes if you should rent your new property. Additionally, on the resale of the newly acquired vacation property, by having a higher basis, you will have less capital gains liability should the resale price exceed $500,000 and the property become your primary residence. However, you may want to consider conveying your vacation home by way of another exchange instead of using a standard sale. If you receive money plus a replacement property or unlike property in an exchange in which you realize gain, you are liable for capital gains tax on the value of the money and unlike property received (e.g., securities). Another variation is where you have exchanged a like-kind property from a relative. These exchanges are permitted by the Tax Code, but both parties to the exchange must retain ownership of their properties for at least two years after the exchange. Otherwise, if the exchange is disqualified due to nonrecognition of tax treatment, any loss or gain from the exchange must be recognized.

Two time limits are critical to an approved like-kind property exchange: (1) the property to be exchanged must be *identified within 45 days* after the date you transfer the property given up in the exchange and (2) the exchanged property must be received (transaction must be closed) the earlier of (a) 180 days after the date on which your exchanged property is given up or (b) the due date, including extensions, for your tax return in the year that the like-kind exchange occurs. It probably is wise to avoid new construction for an exchange since there may be insufficient time to complete the transaction within the 45- and 180-day periods. Winter weather, as well as an extremely wet spring season, may delay construction.

What will be the amount of depreciable real estate once a deferred property exchange has occurred? (See the "Depreciation" section in Chapter 15.) Assume that the relinquished property sells for $300,000, the adjusted basis is $200,000, and $400,000 boot is paid by the exchanger. Then, the adjusted basis, which can be depreciated in the replacement property, is $700,000 less its land value of say $250,000, or $450,000. The amount of boot may be in the form of cash or mortgage debt or some combination of each.

In deferred property exchange transactions, a potentially lower basis may be transferred from the relinquished property to the replacement property. If so, there will be more gain and tax liability when the replacement (acquired) property is eventually sold. However, this tax can be deferred by exchanging out of the vacation property later for another property. Once it goes into the taxpayer's estate, no capital gains tax is due since the basis is then adjusted up to the market value of the property at that time.

An exchanger may identify the following:

1. Up to three replacement properties without regard to their value,

2. Any number of properties as long as the aggregate market value of the identified properties does not exceed 200 percent of the aggregate value of the relinquished properties, or

3. Any number of properties without regard to the aggregate market value of all identified properties if the exchanger receives 95 percent of the aggregate value of the identified replacement properties prior to the lapse of the 180 days.

If you are planning to exchange another property for a resort property, then the following phrasing in the listing agreement may be advisable: "Seller is not obligated to pay a sales commission if purchaser is not willing or able to enter into an exchange agreement that is acceptable to seller or if an acceptable exchange property cannot be located within _____ days (or by a specified date)."

Prior to initiating a deferred property exchange, it would be wise to retain legal and tax counsel as well as an experienced qualified intermediary. Language should be used in a purchase contract (1) to establish intent to transfer property via a Section 1031 tax-deferred exchange, (2) to release the buyer from any liabilities related to the exchange, and (3) to notify the buyer in writing of assignment of the sales contract. Language similar to the following should suffice in accomplishing these three objectives.

Buyer is aware that Seller intends to perform an IRC §1031 tax-deferred exchange. Seller requests buyer's cooperation in such an exchange, and agrees to hold buyer harmless from any and all claims, liabilities, costs, or delays in time resulting from the exchange. Buyer agrees to an assignment of this contract by the seller.

Qualifying a Property for Exchange

In order for a property to be eligible for a *like-kind* property exchange, it must have been held as an investment or for productive use in a trade or business. In this regard, a vacation home may qualify as an investment property, but your *primary personal residence or dealer property does not qualify*. A dealer property is one that is acquired for resale. If you have a history of "flipping" properties, that is, holding for a short period and then reselling them or buying and selling properties on a regular basis, you may be viewed as a dealer. The IRS cannot look into the mind of a taxpayer to determine intent so it has to rely on the facts surrounding a tax-deferred exchange. Therefore, if you wish to qualify going in and coming out of an exchange, it would be prudent to rent the property, use a rental management company, and even charge off depreciation.[41] It would be helpful if the number of days rented annually approximated the number typical in a particular market. That is, if the rental season is about 100 days, your property should have rented for a similar number of days—certainly not 10 or 20 days. Finally, personal use of the property should be held to a minimum. According to Long and Foster, ". . . a taxpayer who uses a vacation home more than incidentally *during the taxable year of the exchange* is probably not holding it for investment for the purposes of Section 1031." Further, it ". . . should rent the property at fair market rental at least during the year in which the exchange occurs and probably longer."[42]

Long and Foster also observe, "A profitable sale must be the predominant motive and not the secondary motive" of holding an investment property. It is well established that many second home areas have enjoyed rising values, and investors often buy homes in such areas in anticipation of future appreciation. Another caveat offered by these authors is, "The Service has also ruled that the use of a property ten days per year for maintenance purposes will not disallow an exchange."[43]

In order for an exchange to qualify for 100 percent capital gains tax deferral, the exchanger must (1) reinvest all net exchange proceeds and (2) acquire property with the same or greater debt. Any deficiency in the latter can be made up by paying boot or cash to offset the dollar amount of this difference.

---

[41] Jeremiah M. Long and Mary Foster, *Tax-Free Exchanges Under § 1031* (St. Paul, MN: West Group, 2001), Chapter 2, p. 22.

[42] Long and Foster, Chapter 2, p. 22.

[43] Long and Foster, Chapter 2, p. 22.

OUTRIGHT SALE OF PRINCIPAL RESIDENCE OR OTHER PROPERTY

If you are retiring and do not have a property to exchange for a vacation property, lack liquid assets, or even prefer not to use these assets to acquire a retirement home, there still is a way to buy the home. The Taxpayer Relief Act of 1997 (covered in Internal Revenue Code Section 121) allows couples filing a joint tax return to exclude up to $500,000 of capital gains on the sale of their principal residence. Single persons may exclude up to $250,000.

Any gains in excess of $500,000 for couples or $250,000 for individual tax filers are taxed at 20 percent. A qualified residence must have been a primary residence for the tax filer for both spouses during two of the last five years. This exclusion may be taken once every two years. Vacation homes are not eligible for this exclusion. But, if it becomes your retirement home and primary residence, this exclusion is available. Also, keep in mind that if a property was used for rental and as a principal residence, such as a duplex, any depreciation taken after May 7, 1997, must be recognized in the sales price. That is, it reduces the depreciable basis, which in turn increases the amount of the capital gains tax that is due.

Two potentially helpful sources of information on markets, mortgage rates, and buying and selling trends are the *International Real Estate Digest* **(http://www.ired.com)** and *Inman News Service* **(http://www. inman.com)**. Also, *Realty Times* **(http://www.realtytimes.com)** offers community profiles, news, and advice to consumers.

12 FINANCING THE PURCHASE

Start with your real estate agent to locate a home loan. She is familiar with local lenders who make resort property loans, their underwriting standards, and loan interest rates and terms. If you are not satisfied with the results, check out some lenders yourself, including any bank branches that you deal with in your hometown.

FHA and VA loans are not designed for vacation property ownership. FHA-insured loans are intended to promote primary homeownership rather than vacation homeownership. Similarly, VA-guaranteed loans were created to provide primary housing to current and former service personnel.

As a rule, it is preferable to obtain financing from a local mortgage lender and to consult a local closing attorney who will be familiar with local laws, ordinances, condominium regulations, and flood insurance requirements. You may gain an advantage by using a regional or national bank with which you have established a strong business relationship in your home community.

How Loans Differ for Second Homes

Generally, a borrower can obtain similar, but slightly less favorable, loan terms for a vacation home than for a principal residence. For example, for a 90 percent loan-to-value ratio loan, you may expect to pay 50 to 100 basis points[44] higher interest rate than for a primary home loan and perhaps 25 to 50 basis points higher for an 80 percent loan. Some lenders may require as much as a 30 to 40 percent down payment for a vacation property. However, in competitive markets, a financially strong borrower may be able to secure the same terms for a vacation property as for a principal residence. Your real estate agent is an excellent source for leads on favorable mortgage loan interest rates and terms. Lenders tend to regard a second home as investment property when an applicant needs rental income from the vacation property to service the loan. In turn, the loan terms become less favorable. If the rental income is not needed to repay any part of the loan, there should be no difference in loan terms whether it is solely occupied by the owner, family, and friends or is rented occasionally. The amount of the mortgage payments on the primary residence probably will be included in the expense analysis when underwriting the second home loan, which may result in a smaller loan.

Buying at Different Ages

As we progress from starting our careers to the "Golden Years" of retirement, both our leisure-time needs and financial circumstances change. Early in our careers, we typically have little cash and often sizeable college, automobile, and apartment furnishing loans to repay. So the chances of buying a vacation property are fairly limited. After we have retired some of these debts, one option is to buy a vacation time-share or to partner with some friends to buy a vacation property. Remember, a time-share invariably will decrease in value. At this stage, you can likely only afford the minimum down payment and want to finance over the longest possible term. A caveat at this stage is to co-invest only with financially responsible and socially compatible people and be prepared to handle periods of negative cash flow.

---

[44] A **basis point** equals one-hundredth of a percent so a 100-basis point change is equal to a change of one percentage point.

Later, as a young married couple, you are overwhelmed with debt. Your best strategy is to either rent a cottage or chalet or hope one of your parents will invite you to vacation with them. After you have paid off some of your early-marriage bills and have your home loan under control, either consider buying a lot for a future home or buy a "starter vacation home," one that is well located and structurally sound but needs some TLC.

After the children have left home (for the last time), you may want to buy a vacation home that all of you can use for family gatherings. At this stage of your life, you can probably afford a larger down payment and a shorter repayment term. Finally, as you approach retirement, you can afford an even larger down payment; if you don't pay all cash, then you probably want to pay off the loan so that when you retire, this second home mortgage is fully paid off. A variation of this plan is to invite your adult children to form an LLC with you and your spouse to buy a property. You may want to either allow them to buy out your interest after several years, or with advice from your accountant or estate planner, gift them a larger interest in the property each year so that eventually they will own it completely.

How Much Home Can You Afford?

The style, size, and location of your prospective vacation home are strongly influenced by the amount of money that you can borrow. Influencing the size of the loan is the borrower's ability or choice of a large down payment, borrower's annual income, and net worth. Other influences on the amount of the loan are whether you can assume an existing loan, use the home equity in your primary residence, pay **discount points** in order to obtain a lower interest rate loan, or choose a fixed rate loan or an adjustable rate loan.

Larger Down Payment or Higher Mortgage Payments?

Generally, fewer vacation home buyers use mortgage financing than do first home buyers (52 versus 94 percent) according to *The 2002 National Association of REALTORS® Profile of Second-Homeowners*. Thus, almost one-half of these sales were all-cash transactions. For the purpose of this chapter, let us assume that you prefer to keep most of your other assets invested and choose to borrow funds to acquire a vacation home.

You should attempt to make a substantial down payment on your vacation property—certainly more than on your primary residence. You will enjoy owning it much more if you don't have to make substantial mortgage payments each month at the expense of other ordinary needs. Try to get a realistic idea of the probable rental income and operating expenses and then finance the property to realize a break-even cash flow. This way the property will carry itself or at least minimize your monthly cash outlay. You definitely don't want to struggle to make the monthly payments, which can quickly change your initially positive attitude of resort homeownership to one of resentment and even prompt an irrational and premature sale of it.

The interest rate generally will be lower for a loan with a larger down payment or a shorter repayment term. These terms may eliminate or minimize the loan discount points as well. The down payment may come from a buyer's savings, securities, the sale of other property (real or personal), a secured or an unsecured loan, or a gift. A lender probably will have a loan applicant sign a verification of deposit (VOD) form. This allows a request to be made that the depository verify the amounts that you have stated in the loan application, so be certain that your reported amounts are correct. The VOD will also indicate any loans made by the depository to you. By analyzing your personal financial statement, credit report, VOD, and perhaps gift letter, the lender can determine if you have sufficient money on hand to make the required down payment and pay the closing costs.

PERSONAL FINANCIAL STATEMENT

Have a current personal financial statement in hand when you apply for a loan. The lender may want you to transfer this information to its own form, but if you already have an updated financial statement, it is relatively easy for you or the lender to transfer the information. A personal financial statement will include your net worth (assets less liabilities) and your annual income. In all probability, the loan will be in both spouses' names so the financial statement in turn should include all parties applying for the loan. An acceptable source of annual income typically is the borrower's most recent IRS Form 1040. Sometimes, the bank will require photocopies of selected pages of your 1040.

Assets are things of value owned by the borrower. Liquid assets, which are fairly easily converted into cash, include cash in savings and checking accounts, bonds and stocks, and the net cash value of life insurance policies. The cash value of an insurance policy should not be confused with the face value of a policy—it is less. **Nonliquid assets,** which cannot readily be converted into cash, include other real property, automobiles, furniture, and personal property.

Liabilities are all outstanding debts. These include charge accounts or outstanding loans from banks, finance companies, or department stores. As a rule, only long-term debts are included as a liability, that is, installment debt with either 10 or 12 months remaining before repayment.

You should be prepared to explain any recent infusions of money into your savings or checking accounts. The lender will want to know if it is from an unsecured loan that could jeopardize the repayment of the resort loan. If this money is from a gift, there should be an accompanying gift letter that covers the following:

1. Amount of the gift.

2. Relationship of recipient and donor, such as daughter and parents.

3. Statement to the effect, "This is an outright gift with no repayment expected or implied either in the form of cash or by future services by the above identified person(s)."

4. Address of the recipient.

5. Date of the agreement.

PREAPPROVAL FOR FINANCING

Preapproval of a loan means that a lender has stated in writing that it is prepared to make a loan to a specific borrower. It will inform you as to the maximum price vacation home you can afford. Some real estate agents wisely won't show homes to prospects that have not done this. Otherwise, you can waste valuable time and money viewing homes that you cannot afford to purchase. When you travel to a distant resort to view homes that you might purchase, you need to be as efficient as possible with your time.

Preapproval further specifies the amount of the loan, the down payment, the repayment term, and interest rate. For example, for a $300,000 house, you could obtain a $240,000 loan for 25 years, with an interest rate of 6 percent. With this written documentation, you know how much house you can afford and the required down payment. Also, of great importance in a hot market where multiple offers may be made on a property, a seller will likely favor your offer since he is assured that you already qualify for a loan. Usually, the lender will require a current appraisal that supports the loan amount and re-verification of the information on the loan application prior to making the loan. The latter requirement is essentially an update to be certain that there have been no adverse changes in your financial situation. A **prequalification agreement** is not nearly as valuable. In it, a lender does not evaluate your credit standing or current debt obligations. Instead, it states that you should be able to buy a home priced at a certain amount based on your earnings. No loan commitment is made by the lender.

CONVENTIONAL LOAN UNDERWRITING GUIDELINES

The following guidelines, frequently used for buying a permanent residence, are also helpful when buying a vacation home:

✦ The sales price should not exceed two to three times a buyer's annual income. This guideline varies with the level of the prospective buyer's assets, outstanding debts, and potential future earning capability. A higher ratio is permitted for a buyer with considerable assets, minimal outstanding debts, and a promising or established career.

✦ Total monthly mortgage payments (principal, interest, hazard and mortgage insurance, real estate taxes, and special assessments) normally should not exceed 25 percent of the buyer's gross income. This gross income is total before-tax income earned by both spouses (or purchasers). Unstable or short-term income is generally disregarded by lenders. Examples of excluded income are overtime income that will cease once a construction project has been completed, sales income that may diminish sharply once a backlog of prospects has been exhausted, or second job income that requires unusually long hours that if continued could jeopardize the home buyer's principal occupation.

✦ Total housing expenses should not exceed 33 percent of the gross income (exclusive of unstable or short-term income). Included in the housing expenses are mortgage payments, real estate taxes, mortgage insurance, average utility costs, estimated maintenance costs, and any special assessments such as sewer or condominium fees.

It is always advisable to have ample cash reserves if there is the prospect of family health problems, if seasonal unemployment is anticipated, if the house needs repairs or modernization, or if rental income falls below the projected level.

A real estate agent will probably pre-qualify you for the purchase of a resort home, but the above guidelines will give you an idea of what you may be able to afford. Keep in mind the fact that you may already be making payments on your primary home mortgage.

Should We Assume the Existing Loan or Obtain a New Loan?

The appeal of assuming, or taking over, an existing mortgage is twofold: (1) the amount of the closing costs is reduced sharply and (2) a lower interest rate loan may generally be obtained. The downside of buying a property with a low interest rate loan is that the lender may not allow it to be assumed—at least not without adjusting the interest rate up to the present level. Interest rates decline as well as rise. An existing mortgage with an interest rate in excess of current mortgage interest rates clearly would be unattractive for a prospective buyer. Initially, a lower interest rate loan may seem attractive, but if it is a mature loan and has been paid down considerably, the difference between its balance (due to the loan being amortized and the property having appreciated) and the home purchase price may be substantial. Thus, the buyer may need to make a sizeable down payment or get a second mortgage (if allowed) to make up part of the difference. Check to see if the lender allows a second mortgage to be used to cover part of the comparatively large down payment. Some mortgages have an acceleration clause which states that the loan balance is due and payable if another loan (i.e., second mortgage) is placed on the property.

Some lenders prohibit an existing mortgage from being assumed. Others require approval of the new borrower and perhaps will raise the interest to match current mortgage rates as well as charge an origination fee as if it were a new loan. When buying a home, it generally is wise to obtain a mortgage that can be readily assumed by a subsequent buyer. This feature can make the property more easily marketable in the future.

Home Equity Loan as a Source of Money

You may want to consider taking money out of the built-up equity in your primary home to buy a vacation home. Generally, you can borrow up to 75 to 80 percent of the appraised value of your primary residence, less the amount of any outstanding mortgage debt. An example is as follows:

Appraised value	$300,000
Loan to value ratio	× 75%
	$225,000
Less mortgage debt	75,000
Maximum equity loan	$150,000

Be cautious in using an equity loan, especially if you are still making mortgage payments on your principal residence and the payments from the equity loan are insufficient to fully cover your second home loan payments. This would leave you with three loan payments. The home equity loan is similar to a second mortgage except the borrower (homeowner) can withdraw prearranged amounts at any time, using a special checking account, ATM, or even a credit card.

An advantage of a home equity loan is that all the interest paid may be deducted for income tax purposes where you may only be able to deduct a part of it if the loan is on a rental vacation property that also is used by the owner. See Chapter 15 for more details on prorating operating expenses for rental vacation property that is occasionally used by an owner.

Pay Points for a Low Interest Rate or No Points and a Higher Rate?

Your first impulse naturally will be to get the lowest interest rate possible. Some lenders permit a choice between a lower interest rate with the prepayment of points (a point is 1 percent of the face amount of the loan that is paid when the property is purchased) or a higher rate and no points. Loan discount points are, in effect, prepaid interest, which increases the lender's yield. The borrower may select one alternative over the other because she is unable to make the larger down payment, including points, or unable to pay the higher interest rate and in turn higher monthly payments.

Consider how long you expect to own the property. If you expect to own it for a short period of time, it may be advantageous to opt for the higher interest loan and avoid paying the lump-sum interest payment (in the form of discount points). You won't have enough time to recoup this initial outlay, which may include a mortgage prepayment penalty as well as the prepaid discount points and other closing costs such as the future real estate commission. An expected longer holding period usually will justify paying the points in order to lower the interest rate and in turn reduce the mortgage payments.

Factors to consider in your choice of these alternatives are the level of monthly payments you are comfortable with and how long you expect to hold the property. Generally, you would pay points to drive down the interest rate if you plan to hold the property for a relatively long term. Suppose that you are offered a $240,000, 25-year loan at 6 percent and no points as well as a 5.5 percent loan plus two discount points. A key question is how long does it take to repay the discount points with the lower interest rate loan. In this example, two points equal $4,800 (2% × $240,000). If the borrower expects to hold the house for over 5.5 years, it would be financially preferable to pay the discount points and choose the lower rate loan. After 5.5 years, he would save $72.51 a month on loan payments. If you think you will sell the property prior to that time and can afford the higher payments with the higher rate loan, then that would be financially more attractive.

In solving this and similar discount point questions, you must first compute the monthly mortgage payments for each loan. They are $1,546.32 for the 6 percent loan and $1,473.81 for the 5.5 percent loan; a difference of $72.51 a month. Dividing this difference into the $4,800 indicates that it will take 66 months or 5.5 years to recoup the discount points through the lower interest rate loan.

FIXED RATE OR ADJUSTABLE RATE LOANS

Fixed rate loans offer the principal advantage of locking in a rate for the full term of a loan. It is wise to use this type of loan when interest rates are low. If possible, you should try to pay a 20 percent down payment rather than a lower amount in order to avoid making monthly private mortgage insurance payments. If the lender permits you to prepay the loan, consider making one extra payment each year. This allows you to pay off the loan perhaps two to three years earlier.

Adjustable rate mortgages, also known as ARMs, permit the interest rate to float in relation to an index such as Treasury securities. They offer lower initial interest rates than fixed-rate loans; they adjust according to a preset schedule, perhaps every one, three, or five years. These loans protect a borrower to a degree against sharp rises in interest rates by having annual caps on interest rate increases and caps for the term of the loan (called a lifetime cap). These loans are attractive when rates are high but are expected to decline in the future. In considering this type of loan, determine if you (1) can convert it to a fixed rate if rates decline in the future and (2) whether the rate index has been relatively stable.

Another type of loan is a combination of the fixed rate and ARM; it is known as a *reset, hybrid,* or *two-step mortgage.* These 30-year loans are available as 5/25 and 7/23 terms. For example, during the first five years of the loan, a convertible loan has a comparatively low fixed interest rate and then converts to a new interest rate (based on the terms of the loan) for the remaining 25 years. Alternatively, a nonconvertible 5/25 loan changes after five or seven years into a one-year ARM that adjusts periodically for the remaining 23 or 25 years.

SHORT- OR LONG-TERM LOAN

It is generally preferable to finance your vacation property over a shorter period rather than a longer period. But like so many real estate investment decisions, the choice depends on a buyer's personal circumstances and the availability of loan terms. For instance, a person with high income or a property with a strong rental history may find it relatively easy to finance over a shorter period. Also, an older couple may desire to pay off a loan prior to retirement. Let's look at an example where the buyer is interested in buying a $300,000 vacation property. Loan terms for a 15-year loan are 5.75 percent interest and no points; a 30-year loan requires a 6.0 percent interest and one discount point. The same 20 percent down payment is required for both loans. The monthly loan payments for the 15- and 30-year loans are $1,992.98 and $1,438.92, respectively. Thus, the 30-year loan is $554.06 less per month. Other considerations are that (1) after the 15-year loan is paid off, the borrower still owes $170,517 on the 30-year loan, (2) the total interest on the 30-year loan is over twice as much as for the 15-year loan ($278,012 versus $118,737), and (3) you can achieve lower loan payments by choosing a longer repayment term.

Risks from Family Member Loans

It may be convenient to borrow some or all of the required down payment from a family member. However, mortgage lenders probably won't allow this as it can jeopardize your repaying the loan since the family loan generally has to be repaid fairly quickly, which increases these installment payments. If allowed by the lender, or alternatively, you are able to borrow the full amount of the required loan from a relative, you should have a loan contract prepared by an attorney. A loan contract should spell out the amount borrowed, interest rate, loan term, monthly installments, and other terms such as prepayment, late payment charges, and foreclosure provisions.

Another option is to use an organization like CircleLending *(http:// www.circlelending.com)*. This Cambridge, Massachusetts-based company charges a one-time fee ranging from $499 to $999 depending on the service required, plus a loan-servicing fee of $10 or $15 monthly. It prepares the loan documents, records and files the deed, and provides payment administration for intra-family home loans. Included in its service is an annual IRS 1098 tax form showing the amount of interest paid. Of particular interest to vacation home borrowers is the fact that it offers a seasonal loan plan where low monthly payments are paid in slow rental months and larger monthly payments are made during high seasons.

The agreed-upon interest rate may have Federal income tax consequences if it either is unstated or below market interest. The IRS requires that for a family loan a minimum interest rate be charged the borrower. This is known as the "applicable Federal rate" which changes monthly. Loans with rates below the applicable Federal rate are called "below market loans." The IRS may treat the interest income from such loans as a gift to the borrower and could subject the lender to payment of income and gift taxes. Below market interest loans involve an imputed transfer of property from the lender to the borrower in an amount equal to the excess of the amount loaned over the present value of all payments required under the loan. If you suspect that you are receiving such a loan, seek tax counsel before finalizing the arrangement.

13 PROTECTING YOUR INVESTMENT

Your vacation property can be a source of pleasure, a place of relaxation, and a sound investment. Therefore, you want to protect it from lawsuits and minimize losses from natural hazards. What kinds of insurance can you obtain for rental oceanfront property, such as flood, homeowners', fire and casualty, and wind? Learn about the various types of insurance and warranties that can protect your resort investment.

SELLER DISCLOSURE STATEMENT

When you have found a property that you wish to acquire, tell the real estate agent that you want to review the seller's disclosure statement. This may accomplish two things. First, it can alert you to have your inspector or specialist pay particular attention to and provide an accurate estimate of the cost to be paid by the seller. Alternatively, the statement can be a basis for your adjusting the price or getting out of the contract. Second, it may provide you with a basis of adjusting your offer for a repair that the seller either should make or credit you if you decide to handle it.

Title Insurance

Title insurance differs from all other forms of insurance; it indemnifies against losses arising from past rather than possible future actions. If, after an examination of the public records, clear title for the property can be established, except for any stated exceptions, a title policy is offered for the property for a one-time premium based on the purchase price of the property. In order to obtain a loan, you typically will have to purchase a lender's title policy to insure the lender's interests.

Title insurance protects property owners from title defects. If someone files a claim against your title, an owner's title insurance policy provides you with a legal defense. If that defense is unsuccessful, then the title insurance company is obligated to reimburse you for the equity in your home up to the face amount of the policy. A title examination by an attorney is not nearly as good as title insurance because the attorney cannot be held liable for any hidden title defect that he fails to discover.

Additionally, an owner's title policy offers protection against financial loss because of errors in the title work or hidden hazards. These hazards may be the result of forgeries, survey errors, insanities, claims by missing heirs, deeds by children, undisclosed easements, secret marriages, false impersonations, unpaid real estate taxes and other prior liens, birth or adoption after the date of a will, undisclosed divorces, title examiner's oversights, and expired powers of attorney.

Hazard Insurance

Hazard insurance is also known as fire and extended insurance or homeowner's insurance. It protects against loss or damages to the building(s) on your property, not the land. Most basic policies cover property losses from any of the following: fire, lightning, explosion, smoke, falling objects such as trees, wind and hail storms, vandalism, water damage from plumbing or water heating systems, and plumbing damage from freezing temperatures. Catalog and film the interior and furnishings in order to have documentation in case of future casualty loss or theft. If you own a condominium, distinguish between its contents (personalty) and real estate.

CONDOMINIUM OWNER'S POLICY

Once the seller has accepted your offer, check the condominium regime documents and speak to the regime manager to determine whether the building fire and hazard insurance policy covers the interior of your condominium home. This would include such items as draperies, cabinets, carpet, and interior walls and ceilings. If not included, you will want to get this coverage.

As a rule, you should obtain personal property (contents) coverage for furnishings, furniture, floor covering, clothing, skis, etc. The rental staff can be helpful in determining this cost—you can figure so much per room, such as $5,000, depending on the room size, age, and quality of furnishings and furniture. If you will have guests or plan to rent the property, you will want liability coverage for personal injury and bodily damage from $300,000 to $1,000,000. The rental agency will probably require this liability insurance. Some rental companies may ask that they be listed as an additional insured, but they should have their own insurance. Moreover, some insurance companies will refuse to include this additional coverage.

Your best bet in getting a condominium owner's insurance policy is to request a rider to your home insurance policy. However, some companies won't provide this coverage if you plan to rent your unit. Another alternative is to request the coverage from your automobile insurance company. They may not be anxious to provide the coverage without providing coverage on your home. If you are turned down, ask for references to companies that provide coverage on seasonal occupancy condominiums. Another excellent source of leads is the resort condominium association manager.

HOME WARRANTIES

The value of a home warranty is no better than the integrity of the service company standing behind it. So, be sure to check with other nearby property owners, rental companies, and perhaps the local better business bureau for recommendations. These warranties typically cost about $500 and may be renewed annually. As a buyer, you should try to have the seller pay the first year's premium. The purpose of having a warranty is to protect you from financial losses should parts of your house break down and require repairs or replacement.

Standard policies generally cover central heat and air conditioning systems, electrical and plumbing systems, water heater, and most major appliances such as the range and oven, refrigerator, dishwasher, clothes washer and dryer, and trash compactor. Some warranties will cover spas, well pumps, and roof leak repair expenses.

Your homeowners' policy does not cover these items. Read the policy to determine exactly what items are covered. Does the policy make provisions to replace a failed system or simply pay for its repairs or possibly provide money toward the purchase of a new appliance or system? You should insure these items through a company that has a relatively high payout ratio, probably over 60 percent.

TERMITE INSPECTION AND WARRANTY

People are most familiar with subterranean termites. Yet, other insects can damage a property. These include powder post beetles, wood boring beetles, and dry wood termites. Termites subsist on cellulose, which is available in wood. Subterranean termites differ from dry wood termites in that they live outside of a house in underground nests, while dry wood termites live in homes that they devour. Termites usually swarm annually for a couple of days. Although the swarmer does not damage wood, this reproductive form of termite is unsettling when seen in a house.

Three basic types of termite warranties are available. None of these guarantees that the termites will never return once eradicated but instead provide for future corrective action by the pest control company (PCO). Most PCOs offer additional inspections for a set number of years at an additional charge if termites are discovered. These are "Retreatment Only" agreements and do not obligate the PCO to repair or replace any damage caused by termites. "Retreatment and Repair" service occurs when a PCO contracts to repair, replace, or correct structural damage up to a specified dollar amount. A "No Guarantee/Warranty" provides for no follow-up retreatment or damage repair service.

As a property owner, you should carefully read and understand any agreement that you consider entering into. If you don't understand any part of the agreement, ASK QUESTIONS! After all, it is your property that you want to protect and it is your money being paid out to obtain this service. Know exactly what service the company will provide and the cost of the ongoing service as spelled out in the written contract, not verbal promises. It is always wise to obtain a termite service that provides for periodic inspections by a licensed pest control operator. To further assure yourself in the selection process, call the local better business bureau about its record on performance and complaints on a service provider.

You can do several things to reduce the likelihood of termite infestation:

✤ If your vacation home is being constructed or newly built, don't allow wood scraps to be buried in the backfill next to the foundation or under porches or decks.

✤ Keep mulch and landscaping away from the siding and keep siding off the ground.

✤ Store firewood away from the house.

✤ Maintain the gutters and downspouts and divert water at least two feet away from the foundation (termites need soil moisture to survive).

✤ Divert air conditioning drainage away from the house; splash blocks can help.

Pest Control

Just what are household pests? Some of the most common include ants, bats, cockroaches, fleas, flies, bees, mice, spiders, millipedes and centipedes, skunks, squirrels, and raccoons. The presence of any of these pests can take some of the pleasure out of your vacation home as well as harm your rental program. Probably ants, household flies, and fleas cause more distress than most other pests. Not only can they be a nuisance, but sometimes they can also cause health problems such as when fleabites become inflected or ants contaminate food. Fire ants, increasingly common in the south, can inflict a painful bite. Household flies need to be eradicated in particular since they feed on decaying organic matter and dung and can deposit these stomach contents on our sandwich or meal. If you place your property in a rental program, you will probably have to hire a pest exterminator to treat your property monthly or quarterly. In fact, you should consider doing this whether you rent the property or not.

FLOOD INSURANCE

Flood insurance is required for properties that are located in areas designated by the Federal Emergency Management Agency (FEMA) as special flood hazard zones. It covers devastation caused by storm water surge, wave wash, or the overflow of any body of water over normally dry land. The amount of coverage is the lesser of the outstanding loan balance or the maximum amount allowed for a property. It would be wise to obtain flood insurance if your property is in a flood-prone area. Such areas are identified on flood insurance rate maps. Information is available from local insurance agents, state departments of insurance, as well as the National Flood Insurance Program (NFIP). You should consider contacting a state agency that can supply shoreline erosion rates (in North Carolina, it is the Division of Coastal Management) or a consultant who analyzes shoreline hazards. Don't be misled about the prospects of the ocean shoreline eroding. In fact, about 90 percent of the U.S. shoreline is eroding from a negligible amount up to 14 feet annually. Also, the coastal population has jumped by 73 percent since 1960.[45]

If the property that you are considering for purchase is ineligible for insurance from the National Flood Insurance Program, try to get coverage from a private insurer. The latter insurer may not always provide flood insurance coverage, however. If available, it may be more expensive than from the NFIP. Be aware that Federal flood insurance covers only the structure and does not cover damage from hurricanes. Lack of Federal flood insurance can make a considerable difference in the value of ocean frontage and limit financing options. For instance, on Topsail Island, North Carolina, oceanfront lots having Federal flood insurance may bring almost twice the price of similar lots lacking this insurance.

A concern in coastal areas is "beach migration," which is generally associated with rising sea levels according to a bulletin entitled "Questions and Answers: Purchasing Coastal Real Estate in North Carolina" by Putnam Real Estate Company in Morehead City. The ocean has risen about six inches during the last century, causing North Carolina's barrier islands to migrate landward. According to the North Carolina Division of Coastal

---

[45] Betty Joyce Nash, "Shrinking Beaches, Swelling Problems," *FRBR: Cross Sections*, Vol. 13, No. 2, p. 1 (http://www.rich.frb.org/pubs/), click list of publications, click Cross Sections, click Summer 1996.

Management, over the past 50 years, there has been an average long-term erosion rate of two to three feet annually.

At the southern end of Virginia Beach is the community of Sandbridge, which periodically has been ravaged by hurricanes and winter storms. It began a beach replenishment program in early 2003 at a cost of $9.5 million. This involved pumping 2 million cubic yards of sand by dredges from shoals off False Cape onto the beach via pipes. This same process was performed just three years earlier when 1.1 million cubic yards of sand were pumped on to the shore. By 2002, all of it had eroded on the southern end with much of it drifting up on the north end of Sandbridge from waves and currents. Some of the latest work was undone by Hurricane Isabel in September 2003.

You should remember several things when buying a second home along the ocean: (1) check the flooding and shoreline migration history, (2) determine whether flood insurance is available and affordable, (3) if building a cottage, locate the dwelling as far landward as legally possible, (4) never disturb the dune system, and (5) select a house built on pilings rather than at ground level.

The maximum amount of Federal flood insurance coverage on a structure is $250,000 and $100,000 for contents. Insurance premiums are affected by such factors as the amount of coverage purchased, age and design of structure, occupancy, location, whether the building is within the flood plain, and its elevation in relation to the base (one-annual-chance) flood elevation (BFE). Property located near the ocean and subject to storm surge and hurricanes has the highest risk for flooding (Zone V). Flood insurance is mandatory in order to obtain a federally backed mortgage loan in this or any special flood hazard zone.

The term "100-year flood" is misleading. Properties located in these special flood hazard areas have a 26 percent chance of suffering flood damage during a 30-year mortgage term. Property located near a river, lake, or stream is probably in an A zone, which is also subject to flooding. If your property is in a B, C, or X zone, it is considered a low-risk area. A typical policy may cost about $1 a day and is available to any property owner located in a community participating in the National Flood Insurance Program.

You should be able to obtain flood insurance through the same agent who provides insurance on your home. If not, you can call the National Flood Insurance Program at 1-888-FLOOD29. Also, you may obtain a list of insurance companies in your state that provide flood insurance by going to *http://www.fema.gov/nfip/answe2d.shtm*.

PROTECT YOUR HOME FROM WATER DAMAGE

Water, whether directly or indirectly, probably causes more damage to vacation homes than any other source. Apart from water damage from extraordinary forces such as floods, snowstorms, and hurricanes, water is a major cause for repairs, replacements, and ongoing maintenance expenses. Water leaks can cause health problems in the form of mold and also renter dissatisfaction. Some of these problems can be avoided, while others can be controlled. One relatively simple preventative step is to periodically replace leaking faucet washers and repair toilet parts. You do not ever want to have an overflowing toilet, especially upstairs. Place a plunger next to each toilet in case of sluggish operations. Also, place a small sign next to the toilet alerting guests not to flush sanitary napkins. You can personally advise family members not to overuse toilet paper—it will surely cause the toilets to overflow. Periodically, you will want to flush a drain cleaner down sluggish pipes. Check bathroom sinks for hair buildup. When you leave the house, it may be wise to turn off the water to the dishwasher and power to the water heater. Post a visible reminder to yourself and guests to turn these on when arriving and off when departing. Another important action to prevent water damage is to install "no burst," braided, stainless steel-reinforced water hoses on the clothes washer. This can greatly reduce the chance of damage from water leaks.

On the exterior, check the perimeter of your house to see if the ground slopes away from the house to deflect rainwater coming off the roof. When soil settles around the house after the foundation has been covered, it is sometimes actually lower than the surrounding yard causing rainwater to drain toward the house rather than away from it. Check the crawl space or basement for dampness. You may need to replace a sump pump or install one. While checking the exterior, check the condition of the roof and the interior for water stains. Also, be certain to keep the gutters and downspouts clear of leaves. Periodically, you may need to paint the inside of the gutters with a rust preventive paint. Check to see if the splash blocks are properly aligned to divert the rainwater away from the house. Continually check your decks and yard for unsecured furniture and umbrellas. During windstorms, these objects may become flying projectiles and break your windows and glass doors. In hurricane zones, it is prudent to have a supply of four-foot by eight-foot sheets of plywood and fasteners to protect your window and door openings from wind and rain damage.

CLEANING SUPPLIES

If you use a rental firm, check with them to determine your responsibility in providing cleaning agents and supplies. You may need to supply toilet tissue, as well as paper and cloth hand towels for the kitchen. You will want to provide the necessary cleaning agents, including dishwasher and clothes washer detergents, a supply of light bulbs, and bed linens along with bath towels unless the rental company does so. Some rental companies advise their clients to remove all cleaning supplies from the house to avoid a lawsuit if someone is injured by any of these agents. If you own a detached dwelling with a fireplace, either the condominium association or you will need to provide firewood and possibly fire starters and matches.

LIMITED LIABILITY COMPANY

A limited liability company offers the advantage of limited legal liability of a corporation. Further, it provides single income taxation similar to a limited partnership. A more detailed discussion of this form of ownership is found in Chapter 8.

14 Leasing Your Property

Rarely will a property's rental revenue offset all of its operating expenses, especially if there is a mortgage on it. Owners of lower-priced properties tend to rely more on rental income to offset expenses than owners of higher-priced properties.

Different people have different rental strategies. Some of our boating friends purchased an ocean property prior to their retirement. Their plan was to aggressively rent it until they retired in order to help offset their mortgage payments. Upon retiring, they will sell their primary home and refurbish the beach property, which then will become their retirement home.

For ski resorts, a core village location generally produces the best rent. Renters want to be near the intermediate slopes and social activities. Barb Cofield of RE/MAX Whistler in British Columbia said, "The first three questions asked by renters are: (1) Is it a ski-in/ski-out property? (2) Does it have a hot tub? (3) Is it in the village, and if not, is there free shuttle service?" Similarly, ocean resort properties either fronting on the beach or

Courtesy of Seaside Vacations, Kitty Hawk, North Carolina.

Figure 14.1
*Private swimming
pool at beach cottage.*

within a five- to ten-minute walk command premium rentals. Longer-term renters favor being near golf courses and away from the village.

Be attuned to what renters want. Don't become complacent. What they expected two or three years ago might change by next rental season. Not only is an easy walking distance to the beach or ski slopes important to your property's successful rental program, but renters want modern appliances, stereos, DVDs, modern furniture, and an adequate number of bathrooms (a good guide is the same number of baths as bedrooms). Hot tubs and, in some large upscale properties, swimming pools are expected (see example of an ocean cottage swimming pool in Figure 14.1). Generally, there is a trend toward more, shorter vacations so you may generate more rentable days by emphasizing three- to four-day rental packages that include weekends. You may need to be prepared to refurbish your property within five years, so be sure to factor this expense into your expense projections.

CHECK RENTAL HISTORY

Generally, the listing agent will have information on the number of days of occupancy and annual rental income, as well as the operating expenses. In resorts with condominiums, information may be available on the average rental income and expenses for the different size residences (most commonly expressed as number of bedrooms). Find out how many days occupancy per year are typical. In beach communities, it may be around 120 days, while in mountain resorts, 80 days may be more typical.

The peak rental seasons are usually reversed for beach and ski resorts. The prime rental rates for beach properties are between June and August, between Labor Day and Memorial Day when schools are on summer break. Lower rental rates and occupancies occur during the shoulder season in May and September. Southern beaches will see rentals spike during college spring breaks. The peak rental season at mountain ski resorts usually is from mid-November through March, with some rentals in the spring and summer. October tends to be a fairly good month (especially weekend rentals) during the colorful fall foliage season. For example, in Vail Valley, fall rental rates may be 10 to 30 percent more than summer rentals. If you have some flexibility in your work schedule, you might use your property frequently during the off-seasons or mid-week during the ski season.

Rent your property during the high season when renters will pay more so you get a higher return on your investment and more rent from tenants to pay toward mortgage payments, real estate taxes, maintenance, condominium fees, etc. Enjoy uncrowded times of the year and moderate weather during the off-season.

As you consider purchasing a vacation home in a resort, remember that the principal benefits will result from future value appreciation and family enjoyment, followed by some rental income that will partially offset the operating expenses. Almost any other type of improved real estate is superior to resort property in providing a tax shelter.

Most properties today are nonsmoking environments. You may think that you can expand the market for your home by allowing smoking. Experience shows that more and more renters, especially those with young children, prefer renting homes that prohibit smoking (and pets as well).

Resort managers have found that properties experience less wear from conference attendees and golfers than families. The first two groups are away from the rental unit most of the day, while families with children may be in and out of the property during the day and generate harder wear. You should check on the minimum age of renters allowed by the management company as well as whether young groups are allowed, and if so, whether adults are required to accompany them.

Vacation properties present a bit of a good news-bad news situation. With the strong demand for purchasing these homes, prices sometimes have risen at unbelievable rates. Rents have not always maintained the same pace. Thus, guest rentals may not cover as much of the cottage or villa's mortgage and other operating expenses as was the case prior to the sharp property price run-up over the past several years.

Acquire Renter List from Seller or Rental Agent

Many firms will provide a list of past renters if the firm is selling the property and previously has managed it for the seller. If the seller indicates that the management service has been satisfactory, it usually makes sense to continue with the same firm and past renters. You can always change firms later.

Property Manager

Ask about the rental company's promotional efforts. For example, does it publish a brochure with property photographs and a description? If so, are pictures and an IPIX virtual tour provided? Does it market via the Internet? Is **travel insurance** provided to renters? (These optional policies, a.k.a. trip cancellation/interruption insurance, cover cancellations due to unforeseen circumstances such as sickness or injury, air carrier delays, stolen passports, or mandatory evacuations caused by hurricanes.) Does the rental service provide owners free telephone block service so that renter calls are not charged to your phone? Do they require a security deposit and provide inspection service immediately upon departure of renters?

Other factors that you should consider when seeking a rental company include the following:

+ Determine if you are required to provide complimentary use of your property without payment to the management company for promotion or benefit of the resort.

+ Find out how many nights per peak rental season you must make available for the rental program and whether your friends or family may use your property during this period.

+ Find out if you are required to pay a departure cleaning and linen fee for all users, including your family and friends. Be certain to alert your "friends" that they should pay this fee in advance. Believe it or not, some people expect you to pay this fee even though you have provided them with free lodging. *Never* allow guests to clean up, wash the linens, make up the beds, replenish the towels, clean the sinks, etc. Nearly always, it won't be done properly. The departure cleanup crew will probably have to do most of it again, and while you have relieved your so-called friends of paying for this service, you definitely will have to pay for it. As one pundit said, "If you think you don't have any friends, just mention that you own a beach or mountain house."

✦ Determine how much public liability insurance you are required to have. It probably will be in the $300,000 to $500,000 range. Some rental companies require as much as $1 million coverage. Smaller firms may expect to be included in your homeowners' policy. Check to determine if your insurer will allow this arrangement and decide whether you even want to allow it.

✦ Have an annual HVAC maintenance contract. Leave the name of the company in clear view for the renters and also give the firm's name to the rental agency. You can expect to get much faster service when you are under a maintenance contract with a firm rather than requesting emergency service as an unknown party. Provide the name of a general maintenance company, or if a reliable firm is not available, leave the names of an electrician, carpenter, and plumber that previously have worked for you. Generally, it is more convenient and possible to achieve greater control over the quality of work by using the management company's maintenance department.

✦ Check the limit for repairs that can be made through the rental agency without contacting you for authorization, perhaps $200–$400 per repair.

✦ Find out whether it is company policy to pool income from properties it manages or whether your property will receive the actual income that it generates.

✦ Determine if an initial setup fee is charged for inspecting your premises, housekeeping setup, and possibly resort setup, plus an initial fee and annual administrative fee. If so, how much are they?

✦ Request an inspection of the premises by each prospective rental company and obtain an estimate of the cost of replacing and upgrading the existing furniture and furnishings in order to be approved for their program. Ask to see their replacement guidelines for such items as carpet, furniture, mattresses, and box springs. Weigh the initial outlay and expense of replacements against the probable net income your property will produce. Does your vacation property justify these expenses? In making this decision, consider the overall likely performance of the management firm, especially the net operating income and care of your property through renter selection, maintenance, and cleanup service.

✤ Make sure you know if the rental company provides a detailed monthly statement showing all rental activity and expenses. How frequently will you receive your net rental checks? It should be every month.

✤ Find out whether you will receive any benefits from the leasing firm. For example, Kiawah Island Resort (South Carolina) rental owner's benefits include greens fees at rates less than half of the normal resort rates, one hour of free tennis court time daily, free bike rentals, and a 15 percent discount on all resort food and beverages.

✤ Ask whether there is a lower commission charged for monthly rentals in the off-season—perhaps 10 to 15 percent versus the peak-season short-term rental commission of three to four times higher.

✤ Strongly consider a rental company that will allow you to rent the property yourself without paying a rental commission. This may be an ideal arrangement if you can generate rentals among acquaintances in your local area. Ideally, you would still be able to use the rental agency's cleaning service. This is preferable to periodically bringing in an unapproved firm. Coordination and service are generally enhanced when the rental company uses its own cleaning staff. When you personally rent the property, get the payment in advance and make arrangements for providing the keys to the renters and having them returned to you upon their departure.

✤ Read the rental agreement to determine how much notice you are required to give the management firm to terminate the rental agreement; it is probably 60 days' written notice.

✤ *Always* reserve your time periods for personal use as far in advance as possible—perhaps as long as a year so you can maximize your rental income. The rental agency will usually work with you on shorter notice if they don't have a party contracted to rent it at the same time. Always alert the leasing firm of your departure so the cleanup crew can come in promptly.

A management firm will be able to set rental rates at a competitive level. Listen to their advice on how to increase the appeal and rentability of your vacation property. Study rental brochures of other agencies and your rental company so you know how much similar properties are being rented for in case your rental firm is off in their rent schedule.

MANAGEMENT COMMISSION

Know exactly what you are getting for the management commission. It may vary from 15 to 60 percent, depending on the locale and extent of services provided. How much and what type of advertising, departure cleaning service, maintenance, and linen service are provided in the fee? How strong is competition from other condos and detached houses and even hotels and time-shares?

The amount of net rental income you will probably receive is of much greater importance than the amount of the rental commission! Typically, off-resort leasing companies charge a lower commission than the resort. Carefully scrutinize the services included in the commission. Outside management companies typically quote their commission on a Plus, Plus contract. While the commission is stated at perhaps 25 to 35 percent versus the resort's fee of 45 to 55 percent, the departure cleaning fee of 10 to 20 percent and possibly credit card commissions of 1.5 to 3.0 percent probably need to be added. Assume, for example, that one company charges 25 percent commission plus a departure cleaning fee of $75 versus another firm which charges a 36 percent commission inclusive of the cleaning fee. Suppose the minimum stay is two nights and nightly rental is $200.00. Thus, the effective rent commission for the first leasing firm is 44 percent (25% + 19%). The rental commission may decline to as low as 10 percent for large, high-rent properties.

Either a leasing firm affiliated with the resort or an off-resort company should have a history of rental performance for your specific property, similar properties, or even properties in your condominium regime. With this information, you can make an informed forecast of the likely rental income that each firm can produce after paying the leasing commissions.

Another important element in renting your vacation property is whether or not a **quality rating system** is used by the leasing firm. Ratings are established by property managers who inspect a property prior to it being admitted into a rental program and then perhaps thereafter on an annual basis. The essence of the rating system is to reward property owners with the best-maintained and attractively furnished homes offering all the expected conveniences with preferential renter referrals. Properties in a rental program may, for example, be ranked from below average to good to excellent or perhaps from one- to five-star. Rental units receiving the highest rankings may be given higher priority in leasing, garner more repeat patronage, and even charged lower rental commissions. The rental

Courtesy of Andrew Darling, Village Realty, Outer Banks, North Carolina.

Figure 14.2
View from cottage overlooking gazebo and ocean.

commission could vary by 10 percentage points between the lowest and highest ranked properties.

Home location can cause different commission charges. In one resort, off-ocean homes require a 10-percentage point higher commission rate than the higher-demand oceanfront homes. Ocean access properties are quite popular, especially if the walking distance is within 250 yards or five to ten minutes (Figure 14.2 shows view from an ocean-front cottage). This distance is of particular importance to families with small children when the parents may be lugging a beach umbrella, toys, towels, beach chairs, and other beach necessities. Provide your cottage with a large, sturdy beach cart for these items. Crossing busy four- to six-lane streets on the way to the beach is not as popular as being housed on the ocean side of such busy streets.

SETTING THE STAGE

Try to inspect competitive properties for decorating and furniture arrangement ideas. You can get many good ideas from viewing properties on rental company Web sites. Light paint colors should be used to make rooms appear larger. Bright white may appear too cold, so use an off-white such as Eggshell, Navajo, or Adobe White. Keep all the rooms the same color if possible, except use a washable semi-gloss in the kitchen and bathroom. Avoid overuse of dark and mismatched furniture, which is unappealing, especially when seen on a rental firm's Web site. Use simple window treatments and avoid clutter. Furniture should be comfortable without appearing massive or out of date. Laminate finishes, if used, should be flawless. Appliances should be modern and without dings, chips, or rust. Inspect floor coverings to be sure that the tile has no large cracks or chips and the grout is intact and free of mildew; carpeting should be free of stains and frayed edges. Make an effort to have matched furniture in the bedrooms. Generally, solid wood headboards are preferable to those made of metal. Position mirrors strategically to make rooms look larger. Acquire paintings and prints to create the desired ambiance. We once bought a mountain home that was furnished with Florida ocean scenes, including a seashell collection. These were systematically replaced with quality prints and photographs depicting local scenes as well as golfing and snow skiing scenes.

For beach properties, use light colors and beach-like furnishings. Quality sheet vinyl and ceramic floor tile are generally preferable to wooden floors and carpets from a maintenance perspective. Hardiplank lap siding and Hardishingle siding offer advantages over wooden siding and especially vinyl siding from an aesthetic and a maintenance point of view. The Hardie fiber-cement siding doesn't crack, is fire resistant, and resists damage from rain, hail, and flying debris. Vinyl siding will melt or burn when exposed to significant heat. Its color cannot be changed, and it becomes brittle in cold weather. Increasingly, owners are replacing wooden decks with a wood-polymer decking material known as Trex (see the appendix for more information). In some climates, fiberglass roofing shingles have become more popular than cedar shake shingles, which can pose a fire hazard unless they have been treated with a fire-retardant chemical.

WELCOME FROM OWNERS

Create a friendly and welcome atmosphere for the renters and make them aware that they are your family's guests by leaving in a conspicuous place (such as on the kitchen counter in an upright plastic picture frame) a one-page personal note. It should begin with a warm welcome and end with your wishes for a pleasant visit and invite them to visit your vacation home again. In the body of the note, offer helpful hints on operating the appliances, locating and using the cutting board in the kitchen, and turning on and off any electrical switches such as the hot water heater circuit breaker. Instruct them on setting the thermostat at the appropriate setting when they depart. In the winter, 55 degrees may be a good setting so the plumbing won't freeze and burst, causing expensive flooding of your and possibly other properties in the same building. Of course, by resetting the thermostat upon departure, your energy bill will be greatly reduced.

Point out how to open and close the damper on the fireplace and indicate the location of the fireplace fan switch, if there is one. If you wish to have the water supply turned on and off, instruct the renters where the water supply valve is located. In order to protect your carpet and furniture from premature fading from the sun's rays, request that the renters, or even better the cleaners, close all blinds and shades when they leave.

Inspect all of the mechanical systems at the beginning of the rental season and also as part of your winterizing procedure. Provide safety helmets for each bicycle. Keep it simple if you are furnishing bicycles. Avoid bikes with gears and select mountain bikes or a similar bicycle (beach cruiser) with balloon tires that can be used on the beach. Keep the water temperature low enough not to scald renters. If you have a hot tub, be certain that operating and safety instructions are clearly posted on the tub. Provide fire extinguishers, smoke detectors, and good lighting outside and on stairways.

LEASE AGREEMENT

If you decide to rent the property yourself, prepare a brief contract to send to the renters. At a minimum, it will identify the property and the lease period, including check-in and check-out times. Further, you will want to cover whether your property is smoke-free and prohibits pets. If you do allow pets, specify type and size as well as the amount of the premium rental for pets. Indicate the amounts of the down payment and final payment and when they are due and whether a security deposit is required and when and under what conditions it will be returned.

Larger homes tend to rent well, and resorts like to have them available for conferences. However, they will likely experience proportionately more wear than smaller units that house couples and small groups. See if your prospective rental company rents to large unrelated groups, such as fraternities and sororities.

HOME EXCHANGING

In addition to using and renting your vacation property, another way to maximize the benefits of owning it is to exchange it for a property in another resort area. After having owned a vacation property for a while, you may long to visit other resorts or countries. Home exchanges provide you with the means to add variety to your vacations, but without using your primary residence to do so. Also, you invariably will have unused time each year at your own vacation property that can provide an excellent trade for you to travel elsewhere. This concept is similar to exchanging a time-share interest in a resort property, but differs in at least three respects. First, you have a wider range than by exchanging a fixed-time, time-share interest since you own all 52 weeks. Of course, if you are renting it or have promised its use to some family members, you must work around those dates. Second, you will need to be more flexible in identifying a time and destination of a vacation property that you wish to use as an exchange home. Third, you must provide information and prepare the exchange agreement that normally would be handled by a leasing firm or time-share company.

Exchange agencies act as the middleman, bringing parties together who want to exchange their primary or vacation homes with other property owners in destinations they wish to visit. The usual means for doing this is to go to an exchange Web site (see several listed in the appendix) and view destinations and properties of interest. You will need to be a member in order to contact other members who have listed their properties. Then you start the process of working out the terms and dates of your respective vacations. Membership cost are nominal—perhaps $50 annually.

If you are willing to loan your automobile to the exchange couple/family, check with your insurance company about any additional liability or expense that you must bear. Likewise, see if they have a vehicle that they can provide while you are using their home. You will need to decide whether a maximum number of miles can be placed on your vehicle and whether teenagers will be allowed to drive your vehicle. Leave the name, address, and phone number of the garage you use in case of a mechanical problem. This arrangement can offer considerable savings to both exchange parties over their renting vehicles. If you cannot make your vehicle available, then give them information on the most convenient rental car location. Similarly, check with your homeowners' insurance agent to be certain that your policy provides coverage for these nonpaying guests.

Other reminders include the following:

✤ Affiliate with an exchange network. (Several firms are identified in the appendix.)

✤ Describe your property, neighborhood, community, and amenities. Be sure to include photographs of your property. Refer to Web sites that can offer additional local information for visitors.

✤ State the times and desired length of stay that you prefer. Always be as flexible as possible or you may never find an exchange partner.

✤ After ironing out the terms and conditions of the exchange, prepare a written agreement signed by both parties to the exchange.

✤ Leave a set of instructions that covers such items as how to operate the mechanical equipment, turn on and off the electric water heater, return the thermostat to the desired position, and close all windows and lock exterior doors upon departure.

✤ Leave emergency and repair service numbers in a conspicuous place.

✤ Provide a "scrapbook" that shows recommended restaurants, supermarkets, places of entertainment, historic places, other points of interest, and maps.

✤ Lock up or store valuables, such as family heirlooms that could be damaged.

✤ Remember your guests don't expect to live out of their suitcases so clear out a closet and several drawers for their personal use; leave a note about which bedroom(s) you have provided this space.

✤ If you have a burglar alarm system, turn it off and advise your guests not to touch the controls.

✤ Clean out the refrigerator except for a few basics to get them started.

✤ Coordinate the exchange with your rental company and give the exchange guests the telephone number and address of the rental company contact person. Of course, alert the rental company that you have guests using the property for a specific time period.

✤ Agree on payment of utilities and telephone bills. The property owner will usually pay the utilities. It should be the same arrangement for both properties.

✤ It is always a nice touch to leave a welcome gift and note of welcome to your exchange guests. Likewise, leave a small "thank you" gift at the end of your visit and leave their vacation or primary home in the same condition as when you arrived.

You should state whether the exchange needs to be simultaneous or not. Also, make it clear whether you allow pets or young children. You will want to paint a vivid word picture of the amenities within the resort community as well as those in your exchange vacation home.

15

FEDERAL INCOME TAX INFLUENCES ON OWNING VACATION PROPERTY

As a vacation homeowner, you are not required by the IRS to report the rental income until total tenant occupancy surpasses 14 days within a given tax year. Your Federal income tax deductions may surpass those allowed for your personal residence. They include such operating expenses as mortgage interest payments, real estate taxes, repairs, management fees, utility bills, condominium fees, marketing expenses, depreciation, and any travel expenses incurred in traveling to and from the vacation property. This travel must relate to work on the property or in meeting with your property manager, contractors, or buying furniture. Also, you may deduct for income tax purposes casualty and theft losses during a given tax year. The rental income and expenses are reported on Schedule E of Form 1040. Be certain to maintain accurate records to support each of these deductions.

PERSONAL USE OF A VACATION RESIDENCE

If you use your property for both rental and personal purposes, then you must divide your expenses between these two uses. The amount of these expenses that the IRS will allow to be charged is limited. If a taxpayer intends to use the property primarily as a residence, then it must be rented for fewer than 15 days or less than 10 percent of the number of days it is rented at a fair rental. If you are able to rent your home for more than 14 days a year and you also use it personally for either 14 days or 10 percent of the total rental days, your home is classified for tax purposes as a "vacation home." After your residence surpasses the 14-day rental limit, all of the rental income must be reported to the IRS. If it is rented for fewer than 14 days during a tax year, the rent is excluded from gross income and rental expenses are not deducted for income tax purposes. A **personal use day** is all or part of a day when the taxpayer and/or family members use the property for personal or recreational uses. It also includes the use of the property donated to a charitable organization. Personal use includes the time that you allow others to use your house without paying a fair market rental. **Fair rental price** is an amount that an unrelated person is willing to pay for your property or a similar property. In comparing rents charged by another property, it is *similar* if it:

✤ is used for the same purpose,

✤ is approximately the same size,

✤ is in approximately the same condition,

✤ has similar furnishings, and

✤ is in a similar location.

You are permitted to charge off mortgage interest and real estate taxes if you don't surpass the 14-day rental threshold.

A personal use day is any day or part of a day where the dwelling is used by the following:

1. The taxpayer or any other person who has an ownership interest in the living unit.

2. Any member of the taxpayer's family or family of any other person having an ownership interest in the unit.

3. Anyone who uses the unit under a reciprocal arrangement, which allows the taxpayer to use some other dwelling unit.

4. Anyone who has not paid a fair rental amount for the unit. This rule provides a convenient reason why you should not charge a below-market rental for the property.

Work Days Excluded from Number of Personal Use Days

The Federal Tax Code allows an owner to repair and maintain a property when it is not being rented and not be counted as "days of personal use." These **work days** are not counted in the expense allocation computation. Family members are allowed to use the property on these days for recreational purposes.

For example, suppose an owner rents a beach cottage during the summer. He spends three days in May working full time to repair winter damage, make replacements, and prepare the cottage for summer rentals. Then, in September, he spends another three full days repairing any damage from the summer, winterizes, and closes the cottage for the winter. These six days do not count as days of personal use.

Allocation of Property Expenses

If your property is used for both rental and personal purposes, the property expenses then must be allocated proportionately. This allocation may be expressed as follows:

$$\text{(Total expenses for the tax year)} \times \frac{\text{(Number of days of rental use)}}{\text{(Total number of days of rental and personal use)}}$$

The amount of deductible operating expenses increases as the ratio of days of rental use to total days of personal and rental use increases. But, you must decide whether cutting back on your personal use defeats the purpose of your having bought the vacation property. An owner, under some circumstances, may do better from a personal enjoyment and tax perspective by not renting the family vacation property. This is especially true when renting shortens the life of the furnishings and causes anxiety and problems in scheduling family usage of the property.

ALLOWABLE RENTAL EXPENSES

If your resort home is rented for 15 days or more in a given year, the owner must report rent revenues on Schedule E along with the expenses allocated. *These expenses cannot be larger than the **net rental revenues** (gross rent minus leasing expenses).* The expenses are deducted in three tiers, either until all of the expenses are exhausted or the total matches the amount of the net rental income. The deduction sequence is: (1) real estate taxes, leasing commissions, and mortgage interest; (2) operating expenses such as insurance, condo fees, utilities, repairs, cable TV, telephone, pest control services, and travel and administrative expenses incurred with property ownership; and (3) depreciation. While annual condominium fees or assessments for the care of the common structural parts may be deducted as operating expenses, special assessments such as for major repairs like a new roof must be depreciated over their useful lives.

Travel expenses may be included as an operating expense when traveling to the vacation property from your primary home in order to collect rent or to manage, conserve, or maintain the property. This expense must be allocated between rental and nonrental activities. You are permitted to either deduct actual expenses or use the standard mile rate of $37^1/_2$ cents per mile (as of 2004).

Expenses paid to secure a mortgage include mortgage commissions, abstract fees, and mortgage (or deed of trust) recording fees. These are capital expenditures and cannot be deducted as interest but can be amortized over the life of the mortgage.

REPAIRS VERSUS CAPITAL IMPROVEMENTS

Repairs may be expensed (that is, charged off as an annual operating expense), while a **capital improvement** must be capitalized (depreciated over the permitted useful life of the improvement). A repair keeps a property in good operating condition without materially increasing the value of the structure or prolonging its life. Examples of repairs include repainting, fixing gutters, fixing leaks, plastering, and replacing carpeting or broken windows. An improvement adds to the value of a property, extends its useful life, or adapts it to new uses. The cost of a repair may be deducted as an operating expense, while an improvement must be depreciated over its useful life.

LIMIT ON DEDUCTIONS

Rental expenses in excess of rental income may not be used to offset income from other sources. However, the excess may be carried forward to the next year and subsequent years subject to the applicable limits. Generally, you cannot deduct losses from rental real estate activities unless you have income from other passive activities where you are not actively engaged in management such as a limited partner. This limitation does not apply if you materially or actively participate in your property's rental activity. If your rental losses are less than $25,000 and you actively participate in the rental activity, the passive activity limits probably do not apply to you. This $25,000 special loss allowance is reduced to zero when the modified adjusted gross income reaches $150,000. In this, and all other income tax matters, seek assistance from a competent tax accountant.

PASSIVE INVESTOR ACTIVITY LIMITS

Active participation occurs when you or your spouse own at least 10 percent of the rental property and you make management decisions in a significant and bona fide sense. Management decisions include approving new tenants, deciding on rental terms, approving expenditures, and other similar decisions. As a rule, you cannot offset income, other than passive income, with losses from passive activities. Real estate rental activities, except for real estate professionals, generally are passive activities.

DEPRECIATION

Depreciation can increase the after-tax income from a rental vacation property, but it also reduces the basis in the property so that when it is sold in the future the capital gains taxes due then are higher than if the property had not been depreciated. Only rental properties may be depreciated for income tax purposes. Since land is viewed as a nonwasting asset, the IRS prohibits it from being depreciated. Only the improvements (building and furnishings) may be depreciated. To determine how much of the purchase price may be assigned to the depreciable structure, you may either rely on the values assigned in a current appraisal report or use the ratio in the current assessment for the purchased property. For example, suppose the property was just purchased for $400,000. The current assessment reveals a total assessed value for the property of $350,000, with $70,000 being the land value and $280,000 being the assessed building value. Applying the assessed value of building to total assessed value (80 percent) ratio to the property's total value of $400,000 indicates a basis for the house of $320,000. It generally is best to deduct depreciation since it reduces your income tax burden throughout the holding period. However, it will have to be recaptured upon the future sale of the property.

Recovery periods for property used in residential rental activities under the most favorable system, general depreciation system, are as follows:

Appliances, such as stoves and refrigerators	5 years
Carpets	5 years
Furniture	5 years
Residential buildings and structural components, such as furnaces, water pipes, venting, etc.	27.5 years

Additions and improvements, such as a new roof, use the same recovery period as that of the property to which the addition or improvement is made.

ADJUSTED COST BASIS

The **adjusted cost basis** is of concern when you sell the property. Essentially, it is the original purchase price, plus capital improvements, less depreciation deductions. The amount of capital gain is minimized when there is a small difference between the adjusted cost basis and the net sales price. Of course, if you can make a large profit on the resale, then you should not be overly concerned about paying a larger capital gains tax.

The following example illustrates how prospective purchasers of a condominium weighed the financial desirability of (1) renting it 83 days through a resort management company, (2) renting for 14 days themselves, or (3) not renting at all and having the property readily available at all times for their family's enjoyment. A 50 percent, loan-to-value, 6 percent, 15-year, $87,500 mortgage is available. Resort rental expenses, except for mortgage interest and real estate taxes, are allocated 55 percent (83/150) and 45 percent (67/150) since it was rented 83 days by the rental company and the owner used it personally for 67 days. Mortgage interest and real estate taxes are deducted on the ratio of rented dates to 365 days, or in this case 23 percent (83/365).

	At 100%	Agency-Rented Amount	Owner-Rented	Not Rented
Rental income	$19,000	$19,000	$ 2,450	$ —
Expenses:				
Mortgage interest	$ 3,711 × 23%*	$ 854	$ 3,711	$ 3,711
Real estate taxes	1,080 × 23%*	248	1,080	1,080
Utilities	1,488 × 55%	818	1,488	1,488
Condo fees	3,600 × 55%	1,980	3,600	3,600
Repairs and maintenance	800 × 55%	440	800	800
Travel	584 × 55%	321		
Property owner's fee	834 × 55%	459	834	834
Rental commission, cleaning, etc.	9,500 × 100%	9,500		
Rental fee	650 × 100%	650		
Total operating expenses	$22,247	$15,270	$ 11,513	$ 11,513
Subtotal	$ (3,247)	$ 3,730	$ (9,063)	$(11,513)
Depreciation		5,041		
Net rental tax income (loss)		$ (1,311)**		
Principal payments	5,149		5,149	5,149
Pretax cash flow	$ (8,396)		$(14,212)	$(16,662)
Tax savings @25%	922		1,198	1,198
Post-tax cash flow	$ (7,474)		$(13,014)	$(15,464)

*If the property qualifies as a second home.

**Deductible expenses are limited to income; a loss of $1,311 is carried over to the subsequent tax year.

The following amounts are deductible on Schedule A: Agency rented, $2,857 for mortgage interest and $832 for real estate taxes; Owner rented, $3,711 for mortgage interest and $1,080 for real estate taxes; Not rented, $3,711 for mortgage interest and $1,080 for real estate taxes.

From both a pretax and post-tax cash flow basis, the owner does better financially by renting the property through a rental firm than self-renting or not renting at all. In this case, the property owners may want to explore alternative management/leasing arrangements since they are paying 55 percent for rent commission, departure cleaning, and rental fee.

The IRS considers a vacation home to be a business subject to loss of the $25,000 deduction. It is almost impossible to demonstrate active participation if a management firm is retained. If, however, you are an active participant, any rental loss can be deducted against nonpassive income up to $25,000, as determined by adjusted gross income. Otherwise, you cannot use the $25,000 deduction.

Keep good records of days spent cleaning, making repairs, and meetings with the property manager and contractors. Retain receipts of purchases and services when you visit property on "work days." This is necessary if you want to avoid having the visit classified for personal usage. A day in which the taxpayer spends at least eight hours engaged in maintenance or repair work is not considered a personal use day even though the taxpayer's companions may enjoy other nonwork activities.

16 | MAXIMIZING SALE PROFIT

Experienced investors often contend that you make money by buying a property right. That is, if you don't buy right, you can't sell right. But diligent ongoing maintenance, upgrading to meet current renter and buyer demands, and skillful management are also important. Build up a strong rent roll to enhance a future sale.

You may be motivated for several reasons to sell your vacation property. Perhaps you have built up considerable equity and now you can buy that dream property with the equity that you have accrued through rising property value and loan amortization, you would like to spend time in another part of the country (or world) or another resort, you have reached a time in life that you want to spend more time near your children or grandchildren, or health conditions require you to sell your resort property.

GETTING YOUR HOME READY FOR SALE

Think of yourself as a prospective purchaser of your vacation home. For the moment, let us assume it is a detached or townhouse dwelling. Imagine a prospect parking her vehicle in front of your home. You want to trace every step that person takes with the sales agent as she approaches your home, walks up to the front door, enters the front hall, and progresses from room to room. Your presale preparation strategy should be to have the buyer enthusiastically nodding approval at each step of her inspection.

+ Your property should have "curb appeal." Make certain that the front yard, or hallway for a condominium, is appealing—the lawn has been trimmed, bushes and hedges cut back, and the borders edged and mulched. Can you easily see the house, or is it obscured by overgrown trees and shrubs? One way to enhance the visibility of the dwelling from the street is to "limb-up" or cut off the lower branches of trees and cut back hedges and foundation plants. This will also improve the lighting of the inside of the house.

+ Freshen the exterior walls either by power washing, bleaching, or painting. Check nearby popular developments and magazines, such as *House and Home, Southern Living,* and *Coastal Living,* for tasteful and popular color selections.

+ Power wash or bleach, re-stain, and seal the deck if it is dirty or faded.

+ The windows should be clean and the window treatments neat, clean, and tasteful.

+ On the interior, test all electrical outlets to assure that they are functioning properly; also, be sure that all light bulbs are working. Check the bathroom and range fans to see that they are working. Replacements are inexpensive. The sound of worn-out bearings alerts a buyer to expect other problems.

+ Either wash or paint the heavy-traffic rooms that show the most wear, using off-white or other neutral colors. I once bought an investment house where the previous owner's budding teenage artists were given free range to express their dubious talent by painting murals in their bedrooms. It took four coats of stain killer to cover up these offensive sights. While at it, check your ceilings for water stains and paint if necessary.

+ Inspect your floors to see if you need to freshen them. If your carpets are salvageable, hire a professional cleaner to work on them. Pet stains and odors may need to be removed. You may even find that carpeting in some rooms or on the stairway needs to be deodorized or replaced. Smoke odors may need to be purged, too.

+ Keep your pets, dogs in particular, either out of the house or away from the property during showings. More than one sale has been lost because a dog threatened a prospective buyer.

+ Be absent, or if you must be on the premises during the showings, be unobtrusive when the agent is showing your property to a prospective buyer. Most buyers would prefer for the owner not to be present during their viewing of the home. Go out on the beach (with your cellular telephone) or take a hike on a nearby mountain trail. If the prospect is interested, be available to discuss any questions or react to an offer.

+ Always refer drive-by prospects to the agent for an appointment. They may not be as interested in buying your property as in stealing its contents or even assaulting you.

+ Leave furnishings in the house. A furnished home generally sells more readily than a vacant house since it has an inviting "lived-in" quality. Prospective buyers can more easily visualize themselves occupying a furnished dwelling rather than one that is vacant.

+ Make sure the inside is well lighted. In addition to turning on lamps, open all draperies and blinds to windows and sliding doors. This is especially important if closed blinds block striking views. Let the prospect be dazzled by the view as soon as they enter the room.

+ Repair leaking faucets and clean dirty tile grouting.

+ Above all else, give your home the appearance of spaciousness. Start in the attic and haul away things that you no longer need and remove any furniture that crowds a room. It may be a good investment to temporarily rent space at a self-storage facility. Remove clutter from desks, tables, counter tops, refrigerator doors, and pictures, awards, and posters from walls. Cut back on the amount of clothes in your closets. Some of these may be off-season, so you might as well pack and store them now since you will need to do this once you sell the house. Then neatly organize your closets (as well as the kitchen pantry).

+ Repair loose, sagging, or out-of date wallpaper and patch and repaint any holes in the walls. Caulk the shower surrounds and tubs. Replace faucet washers and cover any stains caused by continually leaking faucets. This is especially necessary in areas with high iron content in the water.

✤ Make certain that the heating and air conditioning systems are working properly and the house is at a comfortable temperature when prospects visit your home. If you have a receipt that shows the HVAC has recently been serviced and found to be in sound working condition, give a copy of this to the agent. Locate copies of any warranties on appliances. Provide a list of recent improvements to your property.

✤ Give the agent recent records on heating and utilities expenses and annual real estate taxes and condominium association fees.

✤ Resist pricing your property to "test the market" rather than to sell it. Either have the listing real estate agent or an experienced and properly designated appraiser provide a realistic value estimate of the property. You need a sound estimate that will allow you to sell the property in a reasonable period of time. Overpriced properties will not be shown by some agents or visited by prospective buyers. Demand a *realistic value estimate*. As the property owner, you can decide to offer it at a slightly higher price if you choose.

✤ Plan ahead for the sale of your property. If you have a yard, be certain that the lawn and shrubs are luxurious and well trimmed. Trim your hedges and bushes in advance so they will have had sufficient time to establish new growth. Keep the yard clear of any pet droppings and wallows that your dogs may have dug.

✤ Always let the agent know where you can be reached, especially if you will be away from home on business or a vacation.

✤ Prospects will look in closets, so keep them neat and uncluttered; keep tables clear of dishes, sinks clean, and bedrooms attractive and beds made up if you are vacationing. You may want to consider leaving some weekends open during peak seasons if you are trying to sell at those times. Try to accommodate prospects whenever possible.

TIMING THE SALE

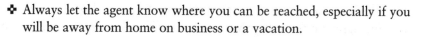

After having prepared your property to enhance its appeal to prospective purchasers, attention must be given to maximizing its market exposure. If the market presently is glutted with similar properties for sale, you may want to delay the sale of your home until there are fewer competitive properties. A key to increasing your chances of selling it as quickly and at the highest price is to offer it when there is maximum home-buyer traffic. That generally is in the period immediately preceding the peak tourist season. So, for a beach property, you would want to offer it in the spring and into the summer. For a ski area property, you should begin selling it in the fall and continue into the winter until it has sold. The pre-season is when prospective buyers are thinking about buying and want to have possession to enjoy it during the most appealing season.

Encourage the Buyer to Make the First Offer

You may not have listed your property for sale, but the thought has entered your mind. Perhaps you have been thinking of buying a smaller or larger property, one with a different view or amenities, or even one in another resort. How would you handle a prospective buyer appearing on your doorstep or calling on the telephone and asking, "Do you want to sell your property"? By all means, don't quote a price, especially if you haven't given it any thought or are out of touch with prices that similar properties are commanding. If you do so, you inadvertently have set the upper price limit. Have an idea of how much you would take and tell the prospective buyer that since he raised the issue, it is up to him to make a serious offer. If he pretends to be unaware of the value of your property, you might respond that you aren't particularly interested in selling and would only do so if the offering price were sufficiently high to justify your considering his offer. If he makes an oral offer and it appears reasonable, have him prepare a written offer on the spot that you will consider over the next couple of days. Be certain to obtain his address, place of employment, and telephone number.

Retain a Broker or Sell the Home Yourself?

Persons involved in selling their homes often ask, "Why should I pay someone else to sell my home?" This query made prior to trying to sell the home often is followed by the sorrowful question later, "Why didn't I engage a broker to sell my house?" I have advised numerous homeowners to carefully consider the following advice when contemplating the sale of their residence.

Determine the value of your property. Frequently, its value bears little relationship to the price initially sought by an owner. You will suffer financially if you either underprice or overprice your vacation home. Your agent may recommend that you obtain a professionally prepared appraisal report, or she will prepare a comparative market analysis, showing the comparable sales used to reach her recommended listing price.

Aggravation of owners selling their home. With the strong upsurge in demand for resort properties over the past several years, many owners are trying to obtain an inflated price while "saving" a broker's commission in order to maximize the net price that they receive. If the sale of their primary residence is delayed by its being overpriced or their inexperience, they may (1) have to obtain expensive interim financing to make the down payment on the new vacation home plus pay two mortgage payments or (2) lose possession of the vacation house while being liable for the sales commission.

The dilemma created by a seller bypassing a broker is that the prospective buyer is similarly motivated to save money. That is, both parties are trying to gain from the broker's absence. The seller, by substituting his efforts, tries to save the expense of the broker's commission, while the buyer expects a lower price since no broker is involved. The negotiations can easily break down without the services of a trained third-party negotiator. Also, the buyer may take advantage of the seller by being a stronger negotiator or by having greater knowledge of real estate transactions.

ADVANTAGES OF USING A BROKER

A broker can be expected to establish a fair sales price. Since a broker receives no commission until the property is sold, it is to his advantage to avoid overpricing the property and in turn impairing its sale. It may be advisable to have an appraiser give you an independent estimate of the property's value. Similarly, you should interview several agents before listing your home. Ask about their sales performance, experience selling in this development, and their recommended price (showing you the comparable sales they used to reach this conclusion).

A broker is able to find qualified buyers. His many contacts and advertising and marketing know-how, especially if he is a member of a local multiple listing service (MLS), can produce a large number of prospective buyers. Also, you will be relieved of showing the property to "lookers" or persons who cannot qualify to purchase the property or are not seriously interested in buying it. Your privacy will be protected by the broker showing the property only at times convenient to you or renters and in answering the many inquiries that may come at inconvenient times for a home seller. Another consideration is the safeguard of the broker warding off potential burglars who may inspect your home in anticipation of stealing your personal valuables or other unknown people who may threaten the personal safety of a woman or juvenile alone in the house.

The broker can obtain financing for the buyer, point out desired features of the home and its location, counter objections by prospective buyers, and deal impersonally and professionally with criticisms that may prompt a homeowner to overreact and jeopardize consummation of a sale. The broker, through training and experience, has become a capable negotiator. A good broker (or agent) is prepared to keep all aspects of the transaction moving smoothly toward a timely transfer of the home. Remember, the broker pays for advertising the property and does not recoup this or other expenses until it has been sold.

Listen to your broker or agent on preparing your property for resale. Ben Hermandez of Mountain Area Realty near Wintergreen Resort in Virginia advised a seller to paint the interior and replace some furniture in strategic places. These fairly modest improvements resulted in nearly a $20,000 higher sales price. People are attracted to neat, up-to-date furnishings. They like the idea of being able to move in and immediately begin enjoying the beach, river, or ski slopes.

SHOULD WE USE A REALTOR®?

All real estate brokers are licensed by state regulatory agencies, such as real estate commissions, but not all brokers are REALTORS®. Using a REALTOR® in handling a sales transaction offers both the seller and buyer the protection of supervision by a state real estate commission as well as adherence to a strict Code of Ethics of the National Association of REALTORS® (NAR). Membership in the NAR is an indication of a broker's serious commitment to provide professional service to persons interested either in buying or selling real estate. Even with the assurance of the broker belonging to the NAR, you should still ascertain that he or she can provide the particular competency that you desire.

In your haste to sell your resort property, you may acquiesce to allowing the buyer to occupy the property prior to closing. This mistake too often works against the seller's financial interests. The would-be buyer, suddenly on the day of closing, may introduce new demands for repairs, replacements, and price reduction. The sale may fail to materialize, or if so, at the expense of badly strained feelings between the two parties. You may have lost other serious, qualified buyers. Also, regaining prompt possession of the property may be a problem as well as the burden and expense of repairing the damage caused by the would-be buyer.

It is far better to sell your vacation home before buying a replacement or upgraded home. You are in a stronger bargaining position and can avert damage that could be caused by vandalism or frozen pipes in an empty, unheated house. In order to avoid these problems, allow sufficient time to sell your resort home.

SELLER'S AGENT

Usually, when a person sells a house, he or she signs a listing agreement with a real estate brokerage firm and is then represented in the transaction by a **seller's agent**. This agent will cooperate with other agents in order to market your property. Once you have signed the listing agreement, the firm and its agents may not divulge any confidential information about you to other prospective buyers or their agents without your permission. This agreement must state the amount or method of determining the commission or fee and whether you will allow the listing firm to share its commission with agents representing the buyer. You should expect the listing agent to perform the following services for you:

✤ Help you price the property,

✤ Advertise and market your property,

✤ Give you all required property disclosure forms,

✤ Negotiate the best possible price and terms,

✤ Review all written offers with you, and

✤ Otherwise promote your interests.

DUAL AGENT

A **dual agency** relationship, according to the North Carolina Real Estate Commission, is most likely to occur if an agent working for your listing firm is also working as a buyer's agent with a prospective buyer of your property. If so, your agent should ask you to sign a separate agreement to permit him to act as agent for both you and the buyer. Unquestionably, a dual agent is expected to treat both buyer and seller fairly. Remember since a dual agent's loyalty is divided between parties with competing interests, you must clearly understand your relationship with the agent and what the agent will do for you in this transaction.

AVOIDING CAPITAL GAINS ON SALE OF PROPERTY

Since Congress passed The Taxpayer Relief Act of 1997, a married couple who files a joint income tax statement can sell their primary residence without paying a capital gains tax of 20 percent on the first $500,000 of the sales price. Single persons can exempt up to $250,000 in capital gains. The price of the "new" property may be the same or different from the sold property with no tax consequence. To qualify under this tax provision, a seller must have: (1) occupied their sale home as a primary residence for at least *two* of the past *five* years and (2) two years must have passed since you last used either the $500,000 or $250,000 exemption. Vacation homes and second homes do not qualify, but if you live in a vacation home as your primary residence as described above, it is eligible for either the $250,000 or $500,000 capital gains exclusion. Be certain to maintain detailed records of all capital improvements that can reduce the capital gains tax beyond these profit exemptions.

You can use this provision over and over. Initially, you might sell your home where you've lived and raised your family using one of these exemptions to buy a resort home. You could conceivably use it part time and rent it when you or your family are not using it for a number of years. It probably is not smart to loan it to your friends. After having used it during your retirement years, you may now want to move closer to your children, or for health reasons desire to sell this property. You can again qualify for the capital gains tax exemption on these amounts if you follow the above two guidelines of converting it to your principal residence, which you may have already satisfied in retirement. A **principal residence** is the residence in which a taxpayer resides the greater part of a year. So, you may still have another residence (which you do not have to own, but rent).

EXCHANGING YOUR VACATION INVESTMENT PROPERTY

How you exit ownership in a vacation property is every bit as important as how to acquire it, especially with regard to maximizing your profits and preserving your assets. A detailed discussion of using the tax-deferred exchange of investment property was presented in Chapter 10. It is not necessary for you to become intimately familiar with the technicalities of a Section 1031 tax-deferred property exchange since you will surely seek expert advice on this subject from your tax accountant or an attorney who is conversant with these transactions.

It is of utmost importance that you handle your vacation property correctly in order to assure yourself the optimum exit sales option. The IRS cannot read a taxpayer's mind but can interpret intent by observing the facts of how a property is owned to determine whether it was a personal property or an investment property.

Several things can be done to enhance the probability of your sale qualifying as a tax-deferred exchange. First, treat it as an investment property. Rent it considerably during the peak season and holidays in order to build up the number of rented days in comparison to the typical number of days available in those periods. If, for example, at the resort where your property is located, the occupancy level generally is 40 percent or 144 days, then you should strive to rent your property for at least 120 days. Next, use a rental agent and also attempt to rent it yourself. Keep records of any advertising and related expenses that you paid in renting the property on your own. Make the case that you bought the property as an investment property when you earn a profit on selling it.

A profit can be earned on any investment property in two principal ways. One is to rent it, and the other is to sell it at a profit. Discuss with your tax accountant the relative merits of establishing a depreciation schedule for the property. You, of course, can only depreciate an investment property so this would strengthen your position in having bought it for investment purposes. You may decide not to do so in order to maximize your basis in a future exchange. You may exchange for any type of investment, including another vacation property, or maybe you are at the stage of life where you prefer a typical income-producing property such as an office building.

Appendix

Contacts

American Resort Development Association,
http://www.arda.org, 1220 L Street, NW
Washington, DC 20005 (202) 371–6700.

American Society of Home Inspectors,
http://www. ashi.com. Locate a member in your
locale by calling 1–800–743–2744.

Asset Preservation, Inc.,
http://www.apiexchange.com, is a national
"qualified intermediary" company whose purpose is to guide an investor through a § 1031
exchange by providing information on exchange
requirements, produce the necessary exchange
documents, and manage their funds.

CircleLending, http://www.circlelending.com, is a
firm that prepares loan documents, records
and files the deed, and provides payment
administration for noninstitutional loans.

Coastal Living,
http://www.coastallivinghomefinder.com, view
coastal developments in specific areas and
coastal homes and home sites for sale in the
United States and Canada.

E-Loan, http://www.eloan.com, may be used to
calculate monthly mortgage payments and
amortization at different down payments and
purchase prices. Near the bottom of the screen,
click on "Tools," "Mortgage Calculator," then
"Payment Calculator."

HardiPlank, http://www.jameshardie.com (1–800–
9HARDIE), this durable, low-maintenance
fiber-cement siding does not crack, is fire
resistant, and resists damage from rain, hail,
and flying debris.

Inman News Service, http://www.inman.com,
provides news on markets, mortgage rates,
and buying and selling trends.

Internal Revenue Service, http://www.irs.gov, for
tax questions call 1–800–829–1040 or make an
appointment at your local IRS office to arrange
an in-person appointment.

International Real Estate Digest,
http://www.ired. com, offers links to
worldwide real estate Internet sites; lists
foreclosure (fee charged) and information
of local REALTOR® associations.

Internet search engines, such as AltaVista, Dogpile,
Excite, Google, Webcrawler, and Yahoo, can
provide a variety of information by entering
key words.

National Association of Exclusive Buyer Agents,
http://www.naeba.org, (407) 767–7700 provides
a directory of exclusive buyer agents.

National Association of Homebuilders,
http://www.homebuilder.com, has listings on
newly built homes by community.

National Association of REALTORS®,
http://www. realtor.com, provides both
new and previously owned home listings,
including pictures and virtual tours.

Old House Web, http://www.oldhouseweb.net, offers
a variety of valuable information, including
product spotlight, guide to suppliers, yard and
garden; ask questions and find answers on its
bulletin board, plus over 11,500 house plans on
such categories as seaside cottages and decks.

Real Estate Buyer's Agent Council, Inc.,
http://www.rebac.net, is an affiliate of the
National Association of REALTORS®; it is
geared toward agents who want to enhance
their buyer representation skills.

Realty Times, http://www.realtytimes.com, offers
community profiles, news, and advice to
consumers. Time-share resales use search
engine; there will be numerous sites to
research.

The Real Estate Library,
http://www.therealestatelibrary.com, provides
foreclosure listings (with limited information),
articles, and resources.

Timeshare Users Group,
http://www.timeshare-users-group.com,
provides time-share advice for members,
newsletters, reviews of time-share resorts;
assists with buying, selling, and trading
properties without commissions.

Trex, http://www.trex.com, is a low-maintenance
wood-polymer decking and railing material
that eliminates the need for staining and sealing
(1–800–BUY–TREX).

Vacation Rental Managers Association (VRMA),
http://www.VRMA.com, for access to directory
for over 500 member firms managing 135,000
properties, contact 1–800–871–8762.

Vacation Home Exchange Agencies

Digsville Home and Hospitality Exchange Club,
http://www.digsville.com, provides description
of property and owner profile.

http://www.seniorhomeexchange.com, is designed
for people over 50 years of age who are more
flexible and tend to take longer vacations.

HomeExchange, Inc.,
http://www.homeexchange.com, provides for

home exchanges, usually at no cost to either party, and vacation rentals.

International Vacation Home Exchange, http://www. onlinehomeexchange.com, no joining fee, can exchange a home for credits and use credits when and where you want to trade.

Intervac Home Exchange, http://www.intervacus.com, is the oldest exchange company with 10,000 listings per year, 80 percent of which are international; offers maps, printed directories, and telephone support in English.

Vacation Homes Unlimited, http://www.exchangehomes.com, has handled the exchange of homes worldwide since 1986.

GLOSSARY

A

Active participation occurs when you or your spouse own at least 10 percent of the rental property and you make management decisions in a significant and bona fide manner.

Adjustable rate mortgages, also known as ARMs, permit the interest rate to float in relation to an index such as Treasury securities.

Adjusted cost basis is of concern when you sell property. It is the original purchase price, plus capital improvements, less depreciation deductions.

Assets are all things of value owned by the borrower.

B

Baby Boomers were born between 1946 and 1964. They are entering the peak age for purchasing vacation homes and are both the largest and wealthiest single population group in history.

Basis point equals one-hundredth of a percent, so a 100-basis point change is equal to a one-percentage point change.

Buyer's agent can help a buyer prepare and submit an offer to the seller. The agent may seek compensation from the buyer if the listing agent refuses to pay.

C

Capital gains tax is payable on the profit from the sale of real estate. It is 20 percent rather than a higher rate applicable to ordinary income.

Capital improvement extends the life of an improvement and must be capitalized (i.e.,

depreciated) over the permitted useful life of the improvement.

Client is a person who has established in writing an agency relationship with the agent and has agreed to be represented by a brokerage company.

Closing takes place when the title to real estate is transferred from a seller to a buyer; the necessary documents are accumulated and funds disbursed, and the deed of trust or mortgage is recorded in the public records.

Comparative market analysis (CMA) is a short report prepared by a real estate agent or broker that includes several recent sales of similar homes along with a suggested listing price for an owner's home.

Counteroffer is a modification of the original offer.

Customer is a person who wants to buy real estate but who has not established an agency relationship and is not represented by an agent.

D

Discount points are prepaid loan interest, which increase the lender's yield.

Dual agency is an agency arrangement that allows an agent or firm to represent both the seller and the buyer.

Due diligence involves performing the necessary investigation to assure that an acquired property is legally, environmentally, and physically sound.

E

Equity buildup begins with the down payment. The amount of equity increases as the value of the property rises and the mortgage balance is reduced (amortized).

F

Fair rental price is an amount that an unrelated person is willing to pay for your property or a similar property.

Fixed rate loans lock in an interest rate for the full term of a loan.

Flip is a short-term hold between purchase and sale of a property where the investor anticipates a quick profit.

Flood insurance is required for properties that are located in areas designated by the Federal Emergency Management Agency (FEMA) as special flood hazard zones. It covers devastation caused by storm water surge, wave wash, or the overflow of a body of water over normally dry land.

Fractional ownership is a form of ownership involving longer periods than possible with time-shares, generally ranging from five to 13 weeks.

Fronts beach road is the property on the opposite side of a road from the beach. Thus, a road must be crossed in order to reach the beach. The number of traffic lanes and volume can affect the appeal of the property.

G

General partnership is one in which each partner is individually liable for all the partnership debt.

Generation X are those Americans who were born between 1965 and 1978.

Getaways are bonus weeks available through exchange companies for time-share owners to purchase time at participating resorts at reduced rates.

Gross income is total before-tax income earned by both spouses (or purchasers).

H

Hazard insurance, also known as fire and extended insurance or homeowners' insurance; it protects against property losses from fire, lightning, explosion, smoke, and falling objects such as trees, wind, and hail storms.

Home equity loan is similar to a second mortgage except the homeowner can withdraw pre-arranged amounts at any time, using a special checking account, ATM, or even a credit card.

HVAC refers to a home's heating, ventilation, and air condition system.

I

Improved real estate is a site with a building on it in contrast to a vacant lot.

Income tax shelter occurs largely through a property being depreciated (cost recovery), which can create an income tax savings.

J

Joint tenancy occurs when real estate is held by two or more persons with each having an equal ownership. If one of the owners dies, the undivided estate passes to the surviving joint tenant(s).

L

Leverage is the result of borrowing capital for an investment. It multiplies financial results, which may be either positive or negative.

Liabilities are all outstanding debts.

Limited liability company (LLC) is a relatively new concept. An LLC can have the same tax flow status of a partnership if certain conditions have been met. It permits single taxation like a partnership and has limited legal liability of a corporation.

Limited partnership is an ownership form where the limited partners have no personal liability to creditors, but the general partner does.

Line of credit is provided by a bank to a customer in the form of a specified loan amount over a given period. It must be collateralized by appropriate assets controlled by the bank until the line of credit is repaid.

Liquid assets are fairly easily converted into cash and include savings and checking accounts, stocks and bonds, and the net cash value of life insurance policies.

Lock-off unit is a time-share unit with at least two bedrooms, kitchen, and kitchenette with each having a separate entrance. An owner can rent one unit and occupy the other or deposit them for exchange as a two-bedroom (or more) unit or two separate one-bedroom (or more) units.

N

Net rental revenues are gross rent minus leasing expenses.

Net worth is the amount that assets exceed liabilities. Assets may be free and clear or encumbered by debt. The cash value of insurance policies, not the much larger face value, is included as an asset. Liquid assets can readily be converted into cash, whereas nonliquid assets cannot easily be converted into cash for the down payment. Included under liabilities are unpaid debts.

NIMBY is also known as "not in my backyard" and is neighborhood resistance to change.

Nonliquid assets cannot readily be converted into cash and include other real property, automobiles, furniture, and personal property.

O

Oceanfront. There are no lots between the property and the beach.

Oceanside. There is no major highway between the property and the beach.

Option gives the option holder the right, but not the obligation, to buy a property at a specified price and within a stated time period.

P

Partnership is an association of two or more persons to conduct business. A major attraction of a partnership is that its income and losses are passed through to the individual partners, avoiding double taxation and sheltering other income through allowable partnership losses.

Personal use day is all or part of a day when the taxpayer and/or family members use the property for personal or recreational uses.

Preapproval of a loan means that a lender has stated in writing that it is prepared to make a loan at a specified maximum amount to a specific borrower.

Pre-qualification agreement is prepared by a lender who states that a prospective owner should be able to buy a home priced at a certain amount based on his earnings, but no loan commitment is made by the lender.

Principal residence is the residence in which a taxpayer resides the greater part of a tax year.

Q

Quality rating system is used by leasing firms to reward property owners with the best-maintained and most attractively furnished homes offering all the expected conveniences with preferential renter referrals.

R

Real estate agent is licensed and regulated by a state board or commission. An agent may either be an employee or independent contractor but works under a broker who generally owns the realty firm.

Real estate broker is licensed and regulated by a state board or commission.

REALTOR® may be either a sales agent or broker, but additionally is subject to the Code of Ethics of the National Association of REALTORS®.

Relinquished property is the property that the taxpayer initially owns and wants to dispose of in a tax-deferred exchange.

Rental income is received from the rent of a vacation property. It typically is earned on a weekly basis during the peak season and monthly in the off season.

Repairs keep a property in good operating condition without materially increasing the value of the structure or prolonging its life; they may be expensed, that is, charged off as an annual operating expense.

Replacement property is the property that the taxpayer receives in a tax-deferred exchange.

Restrictive covenants are established by the developer and later enforced by the property owners within a subdivision. They are intended to protect and maintain a neighborhood's architectural integrity.

Right of first negotiation requires that the owner notify the holder of this right that she intends to sell the property and the two parties have a specified period of time to negotiate a mutually acceptable transfer before it is listed with a broker.

Right of first refusal is an agreement between a property owner and a prospective buyer who has the right to buy the property at the same price and terms that the owner is willing to accept from another prospective buyer.

S

Second home includes both vacation and investment homes, but not a person's primary residence.

Seller's agent represents and receives her commission from the seller in a sales transaction.

Semi-oceanfront. There is one lot or home between the property and the beach; it is sometimes known as ocean view.

Ski-in/ski-out sites generally are defined as those within 50–100 yards of a slope or gondola.

Sound is a long broad inlet of the ocean that generally is parallel to the coast and separates the mainland from the ocean.

"Super Cub" lakes are small lakes that are only safe to operate from with a STOL (short take off and landing) aircraft.

T

Tax-deferred exchange is where a property owner can trade one property for another without having to pay Federal and state income taxes on the transaction.

Tenancy by the entirety is a form of ownership limited to husbands and wives and may be terminated by mutual consent of the spouses. The right of survivorship allows a spouse's interest to be left to the surviving partner.

Tenancy in common involves the ownership of real estate by two or more persons who have separate and possibly unequal interests. There is no right of survivorship, and each person can leave his or her respective interest to an heir rather than a surviving and unrelated owner.

Time-share is also known as a vacation time-share; it involves a property such as a condominium complex being divided into fractional ownership of perhaps one week per year (1/52 share). Each week or share is individually owned.

Title insurance differs from all other forms of insurance; it indemnifies against losses arising from past rather than possible future actions.

Travel insurance is also known as trip cancellation/interruption insurance; it covers cancellations due to unforeseen circumstances such as sickness or injury, air carrier delays, stolen passports, or mandatory evacuations caused by hurricanes.

V

Vacation home is in addition to a person's primary residence. It may either be in a resort or rural area and may be a detached dwelling, townhouse, condominium, and whole or interval ownership.

W

Whole ownership occurs when the property owners own the property in its entirety, that is, all 52 weeks of the year.

Work days. The Federal Tax Code allows an owner to repair and maintain a property when it is not being rented and not count those days as personal use.